FAKE
POLITICS

FAKE
POLITICS

HOW CORPORATE AND GOVERNMENT GROUPS
CREATE AND MAINTAIN A MONOPOLY ON TRUTH

JASON BISNOFF

Skyhorse Publishing

To my wife and parents, family and friends,
your continued support made me believe I could write a book.
I am eternally grateful.

Skyhorse Publishing books may be purchased in bulk at special discounts for sales promotion, corporate gifts, fund-raising, or educational purposes. Special editions can also be created to specifications. For details, contact the Special Sales Department, Skyhorse Publishing, 307 West 36th Street, 11th Floor, New York, NY 10018 or info@skyhorsepublishing.com.

Skyhorse® and Skyhorse Publishing® are registered trademarks of Skyhorse Publishing, Inc.®, a Delaware corporation.

Visit our website at www.skyhorsepublishing.com.

10 9 8 7 6 5 4 3 2 1

Library of Congress Cataloging-in-Publication Data is available on file.

Cover design by Rain Saukas

Print ISBN: 978-1-5107-0547-0
Ebook ISBN: 978-1-5107-0548-7

Printed in the United States of America

CONTENTS

CONTENTS

INTRODUCTION

Politics is messy. Individual votes don't always have an impact, depending on the political leanings of your jurisdiction. There can be an out-of-touch nature to representation, as elected officials spend the majority of their time wooing donors and speaking with other politicians—in capitals or Washington, DC—far from the main streets and townspeople who put them in power and to whom they are beholden.

Politics is also the mechanism by which so much good can come and so many essentials of a dignified existence are met. The US Government grants billions in research money to cure diseases like cancer and AIDS on an annual basis. Federal aid is given to the most vulnerable citizens in the wake of a natural disaster and those who are vulnerable year-round in impoverished regions of the globe. Thousands of children with disease are treated on the government dime through the Children's Health Insurance Program (more commonly known as CHIP) and there are thousands of children and elderly people who live in government subsidized housing.

With all that is at stake resulting from the seventeen trillion dollars in gross domestic product that is the United States government, manipulation of any means can be dangerous.

Grassroots movements represent the pinnacle of the democracy our founding fathers designed, that our citizens deserve, and that benevolent politicians work toward. From those who boycotted buses in Montgomery to those who marched in Selma, grassroots actions in Alabama were integral to the civil rights movement. From tea parties to demonstrations that led to the Boston Massacre, the grassroots actions of a few rebels in Boston helped spark a war that would give the United States its enduring independence. Far more polarizing events are undoubtedly valiant in their commitment to representative democracy. The Bernie Sanders campaign, in the 2016 Democratic primary for president, served as a prime example. Sanders only accepted small donations, amassing seven million individual contributions to his campaign's coffers at an average donation of $27 to give him the bankroll other candidates on both sides of the aisle often raise from major donors at swanky cocktail affairs in the beltway.

These grassroots movements are on unprecedented display in the time since Sanders conceded. In response to the election of Donald Trump, activists on both sides of the aisle (since Trump is uniquely disliked by sects of both Republicans and Democrats) have taken to fighting his agenda with grassroots tactics.

On the left, his fiercest opposition, organizations such as Swing Left, Indivisible, and Knock Every Door have looked to capitalize on an unpopular president and unprecedented engagement evidenced by the Women's March the day after his inauguration among other manifestations to push a fifty state, every district top-to-bottom approach to digging the Democratic party out of the historically deep hole it currently sits in. The results were at first promising with substantial gains to show for efforts in Virginia, New Jersey, and Alabama special elections. They later led to one of the most lopsided midterm defeats in American history in 2018.

Meanwhile, left of Trump and right of center, the defunct campaign of John Kasich has seemingly continued operations unfettered after conceding the Republican nomination to the eventual president.

Right of Trump, and virtually as right as possible, the Trump presidency and specifically figures contained within, including former White House Chief Strategist Steve Bannon and Attorney General Jeff Sessions, have emboldened neo-Nazi and white nationalist groups to ramp up their grassroots movements aimed directly opposite of progress. They have been encouraged out of the shadows of the discourse to be proud and heard in their distasteful beliefs. When the powerful attempt to co-opt and purchase the mobilization and tactics of the grassroots, or a movement altogether, it's referred to as astroturfing.

AstroTurf is one of those terms, like Kleenex or ketchup, that has entered the lexicon as the name for a product while in fact having roots as a branded item. Used interchangeably with the name for what it actually is, artificial turf, it refers to short-pile synthetic turf. The prevalence of artificial turf, and the most well-known make, AstroTurf, on athletic fields nationwide, from MetLife Stadium to local high schools, continues to grow as a cheaper and more easily maintained replacement for natural turf or grass.

The original product was invented in 1965 by Donald Elbert, James Faria, and Robert Wright and patented under the original name "ChemGrass." After its first major exposure at the Houston Astrodome in 1966, it was rebranded to AstroTurf. The technological advancement was a product of the massive agricultural corporation Monsanto. The company is politically polarizing and a major lobbyist along with being a multinational agricultural biotechnology and agrochemical company.

With grass, there is astroturf, a product made specifically to look and feel like real grass while not requiring the care and effort to maintain and sustain. With grassroots movements, there is "astroturfing," the practice favored by those with a political agenda to falsify an organic movement by making their whims and preferences seem like common opinion and desire.

Astroturfing is not only a device used by political campaigns and parties: it is also used by major corporations and big business to push their interests. Very often, astroturfing in politics and in the private sector intersect much more than anyone may realize.

Whatever the cause, astroturfing remains a viable strategy for those in power to foster support that does not in fact exist in hopes of seeing through an agenda. Recently the *Wall Street Journal* uncovered some indicators that could point to ongoing use of the dishonest practice. Former Senators Patrick Toomey (R-Pa.) and Jeff Merkley (D-Ore.) had their identities stolen for comments submitted to the Federal Communications Commission in the lead up to a vote last year by the agency on removing net neutrality rules, according to the Washington Post.[1] This led to a subsequent investigation into the comments by then-New York State Attorney General Eric Schneiderman, finding that up to two million comments were forged. Among the fake identities usurped by whoever posted the comments were a man who had died of cancer and a thirteen-year-old, according to the Post story by Hamza Shaban. As of now that fight remains up in the air with some in Congress hoping to override the FCC through a resolution. That being said, the process by which net neutrality is set to be revoked has been tainted.

FAKE
POLITICS

CHAPTER 1
ASTROTURFED AGENCIES

As the debate waged on in early 2018 about the Federal Communications Commission's (FCC) potential decision to repeal net neutrality rules put in place in 2013 by the Obama administration, a public docket was set up to solicit public comment on the policy. A story by James V. Grimaldi and Paul Overberg detailed the *Wall Street Journal*'s discovery of thousands of counterfeit comments pertaining to that rule and going even further into other federal agencies and other proposed rulemakings. The story says the comments "appear to be stolen identities posted by computers programmed to pile comments onto the dockets."[1]

The *Journal* went on to find almost 7,800 people who claimed comments posted in their name were falsified. The implication spanned several federal agencies but primarily the FCC docket. The fake comments were found on both sides of the debate, both favoring anti-regulation as well as regulation. The posts were made without the permission of those who were named and, in many cases, were unbeknownst to those named.

The public docket is the chief mechanism for the public to participate in federal rulemaking. The legally mandated public-comment process can impact regulations that in turn impact millions of Americans and the decision makers who rule over the process are often not up for election; therefore this comment process is among the only times they hear from the electorate.

Furthermore, to knowingly make "false, fictitious or fraudulent statements" to a US agency is illegal, according to 18 U.S. Code § 1001.

Where the fraudulent slips toward the telltale signs of astroturfing is in the fine print. In many government rulemakings, there are parties on both sides of the divide with much to gain in influence, as well as financially. If you specifically look at the net neutrality debate it is starkly evident. On one side of the fold are major telecommunication companies such as Verizon, AT&T, and Comcast who hold the keys to the internet and stand to gain a laundry list of additional chargeable services if net neutrality is repealed. On the other side of the coin, internet titans like Facebook, Netflix, and Google have benefitted from net neutrality as they have been able to use the freedom of the internet to build powerful corporations.

On the FCC website, the *Journal* found 818,000 identical postings in support of the new policy, effectively superseding and revoking net neutrality. A survey conducted by the *Journal* and Mercury Analytics found that 72 percent of a random sample of 2,757 people with emails used to post those nearly million identical comments had "nothing to do with them."[2] A word-for-word copied comment supporting net neutrality appeared on the FCC website over 300,000 times. The problem spread beyond the FCC and net neutrality to the Consumer Financial Protection Bureau (CFPB), Federal Energy Regulatory Commission (FERC), and Securities and Exchange Commission (SEC). There were instances of people who had nothing to do with the comments or addresses used that were nonexistent. There was even the case of a comment from Donna Duthie of Lake Bluff, Illinois. Duthie had been dead a dozen years. Even the newspaper conducting the survey was not exempt from whatever mechanism was aiming to muddy the democratic waters. One comment filed with the SEC was submitted by "Jason Blake, commentator, *The Wall Street Journal*." It surely was an easy bit of reporting for Grimaldi and Overberg to figure out that the *Journal* has never had an employee with that name.

That comment was removed by the SEC and the commission told the *Journal* that letters that can't be attributed to known people "are assessed during the course of the rule-making process."[3]

A CFPB spokesman offered sentiments of concern for the "inauthentic data" but conceded that they did not ask for personal information necessary to assist in identity authentication, while an FERC spokeswoman offered that those who believe they had been misrepresented in comments should contact the agency. An FCC spokesman said that many of the comments that were fake do not have a substantial impact on rules and that without the resources to investigate, they air on the side of openness to comment.

While the Administrative Procedure Act mandates the aforementioned comment process and also says that the federal agencies need to take the comments under consideration, they do not need to adhere to them or rule based on them. Where the comments can prove most impactful is when regulated entities appeal regulations to a subsequent administration, Congress, or the courts in order to overturn a rule, alter a rule, or slow down the implementation of a rule. They can use a failure to consider comments as an argument in their case and there is precedent for judges to compel an agency to address ignored comments.

Despite the red-handed evidence in other cases contained in this book, where admissions or collective wisdom presented the astroturfing to be a clear, deceptive effort, the net neutrality case only shows a questionable coincidence of motives and actions. That was enough for Grimaldi and Overberg to mention it in their story. The crux of their story found behaviors similar to previous astroturfing efforts:

> But postings the *Journal* uncovered went beyond being merely duplicative. They included comments from stolen e-mail addresses, defunct e-mail accounts, and people who unwittingly gave permission for their

comments to be posted. Hundreds of identities on fake comments were found listed in an online catalog of hacks and breaches.

While many fakes were anti-regulatory, the *Journal* also found pro-regulatory comments on the FCC and FERC websites where people said they didn't post them. In most of those cases, the people surveyed said they agreed with the comments, indicating that while they didn't authorize them, a group or individual might have had their names in a list of like-minded people, possibly from the organization posting it. Some of these people said they were angry that someone who had access to their e-mail address would post it, even though they agreed.[4]

Where there is smoke, there's fire. The largest concentration of fake comments came where the telecom giants met the internet titans all wrapped in a politically divisive and hot-button issue: the FCC and net neutrality. That proposal generated twenty-three million comments, speculated to be "the most a federal agency has received on a rule,"[5] according to the *Journal*. What better place to make an attempt at astroturfing?

The potential abuse of democracy came in the midst of an influx of activity following a segment on the FCC decision on HBO's *Last Week Tonight with John Oliver*. That initial rash of support for the Obama-era policy was followed by an equally fervent backlash against it. The *Journal* spoke to a web programmer, Chris Sinchok, who spotted a "sharp increase" in one specific comment repeating: "The unprecedented regulatory power the Obama administration imposed on the internet is smothering innovation."[6] The duplicates rolled in at a staggering rate of one thousand comments in ten minutes followed by silence. This evoked the imagery of "web robots . . . turning on and off," and led the programmer to say that "many were from hacked accounts."[7]

Sinchok and Fight for the Future, a pro–net neutrality group, wrote about the phenomenon online, hypothesizing that it may have been based on stolen identities. That lead to a criminal investigation by former New York Attorney General Eric Schneiderman in May 2017.

The aforementioned comment and its duplicates exceeded any other comment, according to the *Journal* and Quid Inc., which analyzed the content for them. It had been posted more than 818,000 times on the FCC site. The *Journal* sent surveys to 531,000 of the emails associated with the comments, and the results were curious. Seven thousand emails bounced back from defunct addresses, while 2,757 responded to the survey. Of those who responded, 1,994 said the comment was falsely submitted, a staggering 72 percent fake rate with an estimated margin of error of less than 2 points. As is abundantly clear: "The survey's results, Mercury Analytics CEO Ron Howard said, are 'a very significant indication of fraud.'"[8]

Howard told the *Journal*: "Generating tens and sometimes hundreds of thousands of fake posts on public comment websites for the purpose of swaying public opinion and impacting the opinions of political decision makers is wide-scale not limited to a party, not limited to an issue, and not limited to a social ideology."

Even the vast amount who agreed with the comments that bore their name were upset and disconcerted at the abuse of their identity.

In an examination by the *Journal*, looking at 2.8 million of the 23 million comments, surveys were sent to 956,000 addresses including the aforementioned 531,000 who used the common "unprecedented regulatory power" language. The survey aimed to verify the identities of commenters and was sent out in four groups. The groups opposing regulation had fraud rates of 63 percent, 72 percent, and 80 percent. The only group examined that was pro-regulation was 32 percent fake.

Among 10.1 million comments analyzed by a research firm commissioned by the *Journal*, there were four hundred templates found. Additionally, 1.3 million comments had similar clauses and wording chopped up into different combinations with the same sentiment: against net neutrality.

The *Journal* explained further: "'Tom Wheeler's power grab,' a reference to former FCC Chairman Thomas Wheeler, appeared in 37,531 comments. Praise for the pre-Obama 'light-touch policy' appeared in 68,141. The *Journal* surveyed a random sample of 920 people associated with the 1.3 million cluster; 737, or 80 [percent], said they didn't submit the comments."

This was only the shallow end of the pool. An FCC spokesman told the *Journal* that they received more than 7.5 million comments that used the same short-form letter supporting the current rules from only 45,000 unique email addresses "all generated by a single fake e-mail generator website," according to the spokesman. He added that they also received 400,000 comments in favor of the status quo from an identical Russian email address.

Data analytics firm Emprata analyzed the comments and found 7.75 million comments, or 36 percent, can be attributed to FakeMailGenerator .com, which, quite clearly from its name, creates one-time emails but cannot receive incoming mail. The *Journal* cautioned that that analysis was commissioned by several telecom firms that openly support the Trump administration's proposal. That sample contained a large swath of almost identical comments, a vast majority of which opposed the proposal. The story also quoted the Emprata CEO insisting the study was done in a nonpartisan fashion.

At the time of the *Journal*'s story, December 2017, there were cries for probes, criminal investigations, and any manner of federal oversight or restitution. In June 2018, the rules were officially repealed despite plans from the Government Accountability Office to look into the information-security controls at the FCC and as part of that the internet comment mechanism.

The troubling signs found in the FCC comments were not lost on more powerful persons, with twenty-eight senators writing a letter to the FCC asking for a delay in the net neutrality decision that was not granted despite the senators pointing out how rife with pollution the comment pool was.

The astroturfing efforts extended to other government regulators and regulations being debated. More than four thousand fake comments directed at the CFPB came through IssueHound, which charges interest groups to use its software to bring together people with shared opinions for these types of efforts. However, it is usually with pre-written statements sent to lawmakers or regulators versus comments on a regulation.

Comments on a proposed CFPB payday lending regulation included two hundred thousand comments with more than one hundred sentences each appearing in 350 separate comments. The *Journal* went on to review those comments with 40 percent of survey respondents saying they didn't send the comments that, in the studied comments assessed by Quid, opposed the new regulations.

Ashley Marie Mireles was among those respondents and the *Journal* found that her comment originated from IssueHound and TelltheCFPB .com, a site set up by a payday-lending trade group. Other comments were found with the same origin and falsified identities.

The *Journal* reported: "The payday-lending trade group, Community Financial Services Association of America, used IssueHound and TelltheCFPB .com to send comments on the payday-lending rule, said Dennis Shaul, the group's CEO."[9]

Shaul denied that the effort was anything more than a letter-writing campaign and expressed exasperation and disappointment at the *Journal* findings. The rules are going into place all the same in July 2019.

The same writers at the *Wall Street Journal* found the same suspicious discrepancies in the comments posted about the Department of Labor's proposed fiduciary rule.

Among the thousands of comments to appear were a significant number of fakes, positioned against the proposed rulemaking and aimed at combating conflicts of interest when it came to financial retirement advice.

The rule would require investment advisers who guide retirement accounts to act in the client's best interest. It was proposed during the Obama administration but not scheduled for implementation in full until July 2019, after a delay by the Trump administration. Eventually the rule was nullified in the courts.

An analysis of those comments by the *Journal* found rampant cases similar to the aforementioned foul play in which the comments were not written by those who they were attributed to on the site.

Forty percent of respondents to a survey sent out by the *Journal* and Mercury Analytics said they did not post the comment that had their name, address, phone number, and email. A labor department spokesman responded to the *Journal* saying that they remove incorrect comments when they are brought to their attention and that submitting those fraudulent comments to the federal government is a felony. This finding represented the fifth federal agency to have this fake comment problem.

The task of uncovering the problem is tricky as few federal agencies publish email addresses along with the comments, which makes it difficult to corroborate the sentiments or poke holes in the authenticity. All in all, the CFPB, FERC, SEC, and RCC were wrapped up in the issue. The findings by Grimaldi and Overberg in the *Wall Street Journal* were cited in the Senate when they called for a delay to the net neutrality ruling by the FCC.

For the fiduciary rule there, were also suspects whom would benefit from blurring the lines of support and deep pockets behind those special interests.

The fiduciary rule faced fervent opposition from insurance companies, mutual fund providers, and brokerage firms. They feared its passage would make it difficult to sell financial products with high fees that are good business for their bottom line. This was only worsened by the worries over added costs from procedural, transparency, and reporting requirements. There was concern about financial advisers being deterred from working with investors who only held small savings or low net worth.

This came to a head when the labor department, under the direction of Trump and his deregulatory agenda, pushed the rule back from its original implementation date of January 1, 2019, to July 1, 2019, pending a review of the economic impact.

While the *Journal* could not clarify who was posting the fraudulent comments, there was a lot to be gained by their sentiments being heard.

The *Journal* surveyed 345 commenters among the pool of 3,100-plus comments, specifically targeting those who were, on-face, not affiliated with known stakeholders, including the financial services industry and consumer groups, among others. Most of the comments in that sample were critical of the fiduciary rule.

"Failure to consider comments has become a factor in litigation, with judges sometimes forcing an agency to address comments it ignored," the *Journal* story read.[10]

The results of the survey were compelling, as told by Grimaldi and Overberg: "The analytics firm that helped with the survey had a harsh take adding 'that the practice of submitting comments without the approval of the individuals identified occurs with frequency.'"[11]

George Monbiot has extensively covered the problematic nature of astroturfing with an ever-increasing focus on how the internet and social media have unleashed the potential for these dishonest initiatives.

Monbiot had become associated with his coverage of astroturfing. After a piece in December of 2010, he received correspondence from a whistleblower. The contact had worked for a commercial team paid to find and infiltrate internet forums and comment sections at the behest of corporations to help their cause and argue with the opposition.

The effort described by the self-described whistleblower was complex and coordinated. Using some seventy personal profiles, they posed as the average Joe or Jane to avoid being recognized or spotlighted, as well as to aid in the guise that the corporate-friendly stances were felt by a large and diverse group of citizens:

> The weapon used by both state and corporate players is a technique known as astroturfing. An astroturf campaign is one that mimics spontaneous grassroots [mobilizations] but which has in reality been [organized]. Anyone writing a comment piece in Mandarin critical of the Chinese government, for instance, is likely to be bombarded with abuse by people purporting to be ordinary citizens, upset by the slurs against their country.
>
> But many of them aren't upset: they are members of the 50 Cent Party, so-called because one Chinese government agency pays five mao (half a yuan) for every post its tame commenters write. Teams of these sock-puppets are hired by party leaders to drown out critical voices and derail intelligent debates.[12]

Monbiot dates his knowledge on the subject to just after the new millennium and an investigation undertaken by investigators Andy Rowell and Jonathan Matthews. Rowell and Matthews took interest in a list of comments made by a couple people going by the names Mary Murphy and Andura Smetacek. The aforementioned commenters were entering the fray in a discussion about a scientist's findings on genetically modified plants in Mexico.

That 2002 investigation found that a Mary Murphy–authored message originated with a public relations company with a specialization in lobbying for the internet. Bivings Group was open about the role they played on their site saying, "there are some campaigns where it would be undesirable or even disastrous to let the audience know that your [organization] is directly involved . . . Message boards, chat rooms, and listservs are a great way to anonymously monitor what is being said. Once you are plugged into this world, it is possible to make postings to these outlets that present your position as an uninvolved third party."[13]

Equally transparent were comments on their site from former clients, touting their great business partnership. Among the clientele offering testimonials on the site was a member of the upper management at biotech conglomerate, Monsanto. The glowing recommendation thanked Bivings for "outstanding work."

British Broadcasting Corporation's *Newsnight* program questioned a Bivings executive about the comments and they conceded that it was a Bivings employee or third-party clientele and not Mary Murphy who shared the opinions. Additionally, the Rowell and Matthews investigation, as cited by Monbiot, found that the other commenter, Smetacek, had messages linked to the IP address of the Monsanto headquarters in St. Louis. The creator of astroturf was trying to engage in the political namesake.

This made Monbiot view the comments sections of websites in a different light. He wrote: "Reading comment threads on the *Guardian*'s sites and elsewhere on the web, two patterns jump out at me. The first is that discussions of issues in which there's little money at stake tend to be a lot more [civilized] than debates about issues where companies stand to lose or gain billions: such as climate change, public health and corporate tax avoidance. These are often [characterized] by amazing levels of abuse and disruption."[14]

He goes on to describe the type of comments present on those touchy topics as efforts to "[ensure] that an intelligent discussion is almost impossible—, which appears to be the point." Monbiot continues: "The second pattern is the strong association between this tactic and a certain set of views: pro-corporate, anti-tax, anti-regulation. Both traditional conservatives and traditional progressives tend to be more willing to discuss an issue than these rightwing libertarians, many of whom seek to shut down debate."[15]

Monbiot stops short of saying that comments are a complete paid enterprise but instead characterizes that "efforts to prevent intelligence from blooming seem to be [organized], and that neither website hosts nor other commenters know how to respond."

The efforts and their results are cut and dry in the film *(Astro)Turf Wars* by Taki Oldham. Monbiot breaks down how the film shows the strategies and outcomes. He cites a part of the film in which a conservative libertarian organization called on those present at an event for a covertly recorded training to infiltrate various sites. Monbiot quotes the speaker, Austin James, saying, "Here's what I do. I get on Amazon; I type in 'Liberal books.' I go through and I say 'one star, one star, one star'.' The flipside is you go to a conservative/ libertarian whatever, go to their products and give them five stars . . . This is where your kids get information: Rotten Tomatoes, Flixster. These are places where you can rate movies. So when you type in 'Movies on healthcare,' I don't want Michael Moore's to come up, so I always give it bad ratings. I spend about 30 minutes a day, just click, click, click, click . . . If there's a place to comment, a place to rate, a place to share information, you have to do it. That's how you control the online dialogue and give our ideas a fighting chance."[16]

Just how insidious the situation is comes through when you look at the group hosting the event. American Majority get three-quarters of its funding from the nonprofit Sam Adam Alliance. In the organization's inaugural year, nearly 90 percent of the funding came from a single donation of $3.7 million. That group training right wingers to tip the scales of online opinion was at the whim of a single organization at best and a single soul at worst.

"Every month more evidence piles up, suggesting that online comment threads and forums are being hijacked by people who aren't what they seem," Monbiot wrote in his column in the *Guardian* in February 2011. The anonymity of the web gives companies and governments golden opportunities to run astroturf operations: fake grassroots campaigns that create the impression that large numbers of people are demanding or opposing particular policies. This deception is most likely to occur where the interests of companies or governments come into conflict with the interests of the public."[17]

Around the same time of the 2011 Monbiot dispatch was the release of emails from a US cybersecurity firm named HBGary Federal, which had been obtained by hackers. Those leaks show an operation of stunning technological sophistication and scope being mobilized to dilute First Amendment use by real citizens.

The *Daily Kos* reported on the HBGary leak and that it showed companies using "persona management software" aimed at increasing the effectivity of astroturfing operatives as they work their magic of making a single blade of astroturf appear as though it is a field of grassroots support, creating the appearance of substantial support for corporation's and government's efforts and prerogatives. Additionally, the software gave a realistic, well-rounded personal profile for a commenter with a name, email account (or several), web pages, and social media. Like a real, living, breathing person with an opinion that happens to fall in line with something that could be a boon for a powerful entity. The lines between person and fake profile are blurred. The software kept the fake accounts up-to-date with regular posts of content to keep the ruse believable. At that point humans can join the effort and capitalize on the prepared accounts that already had a well-rounded backstory to work off of with posted links, retweets, and posts dating back months. This made it easier for the blatantly one-sided opinions expressed going forward to seem more believable. Even more effective, according to the *Daily Kos* story, the astroturfers were able to "make it appear as if a persona was actually at a conference and introduce himself/herself to key individuals as part of the exercise . . . There are a variety of social media tricks we can use to add a level of realness to fictitious personas."[18]

Those same leaks found that the United States Air Force was on the search for companies to supply them with that software. With it they planned to create "[ten] personas per user, replete with background, history, supporting details, and cyber presences that are technically, culturally, and geographically consistent . . . Personas must be able to appear to originate in nearly any part of the world and can interact through conventional online services and social media platforms," according to the leaks. Additionally, they will look to give their astroturfers "randomly selected IP addresses through which they can access the internet . . . hiding the existence of the operation."[19]

They also combined the web traffic from the astroturf with the traffic of users not involved in the effort to add cover. Finally, they attempted to use the same IP address to make the comments look like the same people over time, further developing the fake personas.

These leaks, reported by *Daily Kos* and cited by Monbiot, show the real danger of malevolent misdirection that can be created with ease on the internet. Not only is the web in jeopardy of being corrupted, but with the potential uses for which astroturfing can be deployed, democracy and the First Amendment also could be in the crosshairs. Over time, conversations of great importance can be derailed and overwhelmed by armies of astroturf. For all the voices given a platform by the world wide web there are avenues to be exploited by corporate interests, lobbying firms, and bad actors.

Adam Bienkov wrote an article outlining astroturfing for the *Guardian* in early 2012. The idea that a "pro-Kremlin group funded a vast network of online activists to create the illusion of widespread support for Vladimir Putin may seem like a bizarre tale restricted to an authoritarian state," he wrote. But as he cautioned in the piece and is evident in practical research, this is a problem not reserved for third-world or totalitarian nations. With the help of technology, chiefly the internet, and legislation, above all *Citizens United v. FEC*, this is a problem as prevalent as ever and it knows no borders.

Dictatorships may do it with ease due to the ease of restrictions, but the flourishing capitalistic Western states also see this problem due to the vast wealth in the hands of special interests, which is too easily funneled into politics or marketing. It can happen in online surveys or reviews of entertainment but can also be used to combat science and to silence dissent to power.

"Although usually associated with the internet, the practice has been widespread ever since newspaper editors first invented the letters page. Pick up any local paper around the time of an election and you will find multiple letters from 'concerned residents of X' objecting to the disastrous policies of Y. Similarly, concerned residents often turn up on talk radio shows and even in campaign literature," wrote Bienkov. "New forms of software enable any [organization] with the funds and the know-how to conduct astroturfing on a far bigger scale than even the Kremlin could hope for."[20]

Twitter and blogging have given a voice to millions and allowed genuine opposition movements to take their case to the masses. Censorship of these movements has not always proved effective, with only authoritarian governments possessing the means and the will to implement it. For big business and less repressive governments, the alternative of simply crowding out your opposition online must seem a far more attractive prospect. With a few computers and a handful of operatives, whole legions of supporters can be magicked out of thin air, and at a potentially lower cost than the 'hundreds of thousands' allegedly spent in Russia. How widespread these practices are is anyone's guess, but as the size and influence of online debate increases, the demand for such astroturf services will only increase, too.[21]

Dating back to the 2016 US presidential election, it is clear that Russian interests with ties to the Kremlin, and possible nefarious ties stateside, ran a vast effort to undermine the debate and election that is supposed to be decided only by citizens of the United States. They flooded social media sites with messages in support and opposition to both parties and muddied the waters of what was real and fake to the detriment of truth itself. We are still sorting through the fallout and collateral damage to our democracy and the national conversation from that astroturf of historic proportions in the 2016 election. We still have not solved who exactly the benefactors were. That may just be because it is not over.

CHAPTER 2

THE KOCH BROTHERS
AND THE WICHITA TEA PARTY

The Tea Party movement is remarkable in two respects. It is one of the biggest exercises in false consciousness the world has seen—and the biggest Astroturf operation in history," George Monbliot wrote in a 2010 piece in the *Guardian*.[1] "It is mostly composed of passionate, well-meaning people who think they are fighting elite power, unaware that they have been [organized] by the very interests they believe they are confronting."

Over time, it became clear that this movement was funded, established and guided along to the heights of having its own caucus in the United States House of Representatives by the very billionaires and big business interest against which it professed such dislike. Among the architects of this astro-turfing effort were two brothers who run what they call, "the biggest company you've never heard of."

While Barack Obama celebrated his historic inauguration as the forty-fourth president of the United States, his opposition planned their assault on a legacy that had not even begun to take shape. Barack and Michelle Obama, the first lady–elect as of 11 p.m. on November 4, 2008, made their way across the beltway from ballroom to ballroom dancing and smiling in victory. All the while those who wished them ill sat and seethed in the Caucus

Room, a Washington, DC, establishment that would be infamous by the time they filed out some four hours later.

That evening marked a low point for the Republican Party. They had lost the presidential election in the largest popular vote margin since 1988 to a new breed of politician in the ethnically diverse and rhetorically gifted Barack Obama backed by his grassroots-built, social media savvy campaign. To add insult to injury, the whole hill had turned blue that evening with a backlash to the policies and wars of George W. Bush turning the whim of the voters sharply left.

The success of Obama carried down the ballot with Democrats picking up eight seats in the Senate, twenty-one seats in the House of Representatives, an additional Gubernatorial seat, and a majority in six state legislative bodies granting them control of both houses in twenty-seven states. The first African American president would be accompanied by the 111th United States Congress featuring fifty-seven registered Democrats and two independents who caucused with Democrats in the Senate, forming a fifty-nine to forty-one majority and a House featuring 255 Democrats dwarfing their Republican counterparts who held 179 minority seats.

According to an account in the book *Do Not Ask What Good We Do: Inside the U.S. House of Representatives* by Robert Draper, the guest list at the Caucus Room, a swanky steakhouse, included Republican representatives Eric Cantor, Kevin McCarthy, Paul Ryan, Pete Sessions, Jeb Hensarling, Pete Hoekstra, and Dan Lungren, along with senators Jim DeMint, Jon Kyl, Tom Coburn, John Ensign, and Bob Corker.

Though the night began with sulking in defeat, moods shifted by the end as a strategy had been formulated for how best to obstruct the party in power and combat the status quo. Unbeknownst to those in attendance, the most influential and powerful force against the Obama Administration was halfway across the United States in Wichita, Kansas.

Charles and David Koch, or the Koch Brothers as they are often referred, would dig deep into the coffers of their multinational corporation Koch Industries, the second biggest privately owned company in the nation, to create, sustain, and support the Tea Party. That astroturf group would be seen and heard all around the country all the while cloaked in the guise of a grassroots movement. Once they got into office, the Tea Party was professionalized into the House Freedom Caucus. The seats they hold in Congress and corresponding sway on the pace of lawmaking is a crowning achievement for the libertarian political donors in some four decades of covert activism. In the widespread effort leading up to this legitimacy and influence they would cover their tracks through the creation of think tanks, foundations, and political action committees.

At first the Tea Party was taken as a grassroots movement by much of the media, but eventually the truth would come to light and the efforts would be traced back to the brothers from the heartland. By the time President Obama, who they had spent so much effort to resist, was finished with his two terms and on his way out, the cause would be sustained with roughly three dozen members of the House Freedom Caucus. The caucus refuses to reveal its membership but has proven influential in some of the biggest votes in recent history including the controversial passing of the American Healthcare Act in the House of Representatives where they staunchly stood their ground to the right of all other representation in the country. This astroturf has outlasted its intended purpose.

The answer to how the Kochs formulated their beliefs lies with their father. Fred Koch was the founder of the company his sons would eventually rename in his honor as Koch Industries. In 1958, he was among the original members of the John Birch Society, an ultra conservative group with core beliefs in limited government and anti-communism. Their website lists their mission as "to bring about less government . . . The organization's overall goal is to educate the American people about their country and its enemies, in order to protect our freedom and the nation's independence."[2]

Well before his sons would be involved with an agenda accusing the forty-fourth president of secret communist and Islamic agendas, Fred Koch said in a 1963 speech that Communists would one day "infiltrate the highest offices of government in the US until the president is a Communist, unknown to the rest of us."

David Koch recalled inheriting his father's political leanings when he spoke to Brian Doherty, an editor of the libertarian and Koch-funded magazine *Reason* for his book on the history of the libertarian movement *Radicals for Capitalism*: "He was constantly speaking to us children about what was wrong with government . . . It's something I grew up with—a fundamental point of view that big government was bad, and imposition of government controls on our lives and economic fortunes was not good."[3]

Though their backing of the Tea Party was the Kochs' most adept, impactful, and lasting political action, it was not their first. That would come in a far different shape and form just over a decade after the company had been rebranded with their father's name as Charles and David slowly became integral sources of funding for the most stringent sects of American libertarian politics.

In 1979, a thirty-nine-year-old David ran for vice president, joining Ed Clark on the Libertarian ticket to the right of the man who would win that election, Ronald Reagan. Already chief supporters of the Libertarian Party, they conceptualized adding David to the ballot to remove restrictions on campaign donations, according to the most exhaustive piece written on the Kochs to date, *Covert Operations* by Jane Mayer, which appeared in the *New Yorker* on August 30, 2010. According to Mayer's reporting, that effort would cost David two million dollars but would only yield one percent of the vote.

The 1980 campaign would be an early example of what the Tea Party would represent some three decades later. In an event that can be taken as prescient or coincidental, Clark said at the time in an interview with the *Nation* that the Libertarian Party was preparing for "a very big tea party."[4] Among the radical ideas of that cycle featured on Clark and Koch's platform was abolishing the Federal Bureau of Investigation, Central Intelligence Agency, Securities and Exchange Commission, Department of Energy, Social Security, minimum-wage laws, gun control, personal taxes, and corporate income taxes. The Kochs transparent attempt to enact nontraditional ideas into American democracy did not go well, leaving them brainstorming how better to see their concepts come to fruition.

According to Mayer, "A longtime confidant of the Kochs told Doherty that the brothers wanted to 'supply the themes and words for the scripts.' In order to alter the direction of America, they had to 'influence the areas where policy ideas percolate from: academia and think tanks.'"[5]

The 1980 election would be the last time their names would be connected to their messages in such an upfront manner. From that point forward they would opt for the simpler, albeit more expensive, process of laying down astroturf in lieu of the onerous responsibility of planting and caring for grass roots. From the loss to Reagan through the symbolic but perhaps more crushing loss to Obama, they would spend over a hundred million dollars on dozens of organizations designed to appear independent, though conspicuously all drawing similar conclusions to a common end. According to their tax records for 2008, as reported by Mayer, the three principal Koch family foundations poured funds into thirty-four political and policy organizations, several that they directed and three that they founded. This does not even include the millions that went directly to lobbyists, advocacy groups, and political campaigns.

The Kochs' political activities and lobbying efforts peaked as the rise of environmental regulation and awareness corresponded with increased climate change awareness and activism. This cause was ideal for the oil magnates as it not only fit within their libertarian ethos opposing regulation in the free market, but also impacted one of the integral industries within their empire, oil. Eventually those efforts would be channeled through the Tea Party.

This cause created a framework for what would be the Koch's seminal astroturfing effort and the manifestation of the Tea Party in the early Obama years. The company spent at an unparalleled level in the years just before the rise of the Illinois senator. These efforts led to the creation, funding, and inception of a web of think tanks, activist groups, and foundations. The entire expanse would later be dubbed the "Kochtopus," according to Mayer.

In speaking with Mayer, Charles Lewis, founder of the nonpartisan watchdog group Center for Public Integrity, said, "The Kochs are on a whole different level. There's no one else who has spent this much money. The sheer dimension of it is what sets them apart. They have a pattern of law-breaking, political manipulation, and obfuscation. I've been in Washington since Watergate, and I've never seen anything like it. They are the Standard Oil of our times."[6]

The National Committee for Responsive Philanthropy, an independent nonprofit organization founded in 1976, conducted a study in March 2004 titled *Axis of Ideology*, which found that the Kochs directed the seventh, eighth, and thirteenth largest conservative foundations: the Charles G. Koch Charitable Foundation, the David H. Koch Charitable Foundation, and the Claude R. Lambe Charitable Foundation.

The expanse of their network covered a large portion of the study, as expected. At the time of the study, the Koch brothers sat on the boards of the Cato Institute and Citizens for a Sound Economy, as well as its charitable subsidiary, the CSE Foundation, all three of which they founded. The brothers founded the Cato Institute in the 1970s as the first libertarian think tank in the country; even today it is often parroted and sourced by right wing media and politicians. Citizens for a Sound Economy was set up in 1984 by the Kochs who provided nearly eight million dollars in the late eighties and early nineties.

Additionally, they were board members of the Reason Foundation, as well as large supporters of the Competitive Enterprise Institute, the Foundation for Research on Economics and the Environment, the Republican Leadership Program, the American Legislative Exchange Council, the Heritage Foundation, the Hudson Institute, the Competitive Enterprise Institute, and the Pacific Research Institute for Public Policy.

It is not just think tanks and advocacy institutes that are their beneficiaries but also academia. Through their foundations, the Kochs granted more than twenty-three million dollars to George Mason University (GMU) from 1985 to 2002 for its foundation and Institute for Human Studies. In 2001, a three million dollar gift to the university helped create the Interdisciplinary Center for Economic Science and helped fund the Law and Economics Center at the School of Law.

Their principal investment at GMU was the Mercatus Center, a think tank they spent several million dollars to set up in the mid-eighties. The nonprofit research center describes itself as "a university-based research center dedicated to bridging the gap between academic research and public policy problems."[7]

A 2004 piece by Bob Davis in the *Wall Street Journal* said, "When it comes to business regulation in Washington [Mercatus] has become the most important think tank you've never heard of," adding that it "has become a kind of shadow regulatory authority."[8]

"Mercatus's rise owes much to the oil-and-gas company Koch Industries Inc., a privately owned company in Wichita, Kan., that contributes heavily to Republican causes and candidates," Davis said. "Public Citizen, a consumer group founded by Ralph Nader, dismisses Mercatus as 'a wholly owned subsidiary of Koch Industries and other corporate interests.'"[9]

Peter Van Doren, editor of *Regulation Magazine*, which is published by the Cato Institute, said of Mercatus to Davis that it was the "only academically respectable place I know that does what K Street lobbyists do."[10]

The staff and board of the David H. Koch Charitable Foundation gave the largest contribution to Republican political action committees (PACs) and candidates between 1998 and 2003, giving more than $1.75 million. The Cato Institute, CSE, and Reason Foundation were also ranked among the top nonprofit contributors.

Koch Industries gave $1.8 million to support candidates in the 1998, 2000, and 2002 election cycles, all of which were Republicans. For the 2000, 2002, and early stages of the 2004 election cycle, the Koch's own political action committee added an additional $1.6 million, with Koch Industries kicking in $680,000 from 1998 to 2000 in lobbying efforts directly aimed at lawmakers.

Koch foundations contributed to two of their chief subsidiaries, Cato and CSE, more than twelve million dollars each in the years from 1985 and 2002.

In a *Sierra* magazine story from 2002, Curtis Moore said, "Koch money funds industry-friendly messages that fill our airwaves and editorial pages, and influences outcomes in the halls of Congress and courtrooms across the country."[11] Koch-affiliated organizations act as if they are unbiased public-minded associations promoting scientific research and economic independence, yet the entities are simple pawns for industries like that of the Koch brothers.

CSE can't receive foundation grants under current tax law. However, CSE has a charitable subsidiary, the CSE Foundation, which can. So conservative foundations like those associated with Koch Industries make the grants to the Foundation, instead. In 1999, 2000, and 2001, the three Koch foundations contributed nearly $4 million to the CSE "Foundation."

A trial balloon of this strategy came in 1997 when the brothers set up a shell corporation, Triad Management, and a corresponding nonprofit group, the Economic Education Trust, which gave more than three million dollars to help make attack ads in twenty-six states. It prompted a Senate investigation, which revealed they were financed almost entirely by the brothers. The Kochs were testing the waters on how to do the most with the least exposure and create a widespread-seeming movement. Charles Lewis of the Center for Public Integrity was quoted in Mayer's piece describing the event, a harbinger of the larger movement still to come, as "historic. Triad was the first time a major corporation used a cutout."[12]

Just how deep the Kochs reached into their considerable fortune to create and sustain their complex network of influence is unclear. According to tax records from the decade prior to Obama's election, from 1998 to 2008, the bill comes to over a quarter of a billion dollars between the Charles G. Koch Charitable Foundation, David H. Koch Charitable Foundation, Claude R. Lambe Charitable Foundation, Koch Industries, KochPAC, and through personal donations made in their names or the names of family members. This is only the amount that appears on public tax records, and thus, the full extent cannot be known since anonymous personal donations to politically active nonprofit groups are permissible under federal tax law.

Direct donations, be it to lobbyists, political campaigns, or PACs, are only scratching the surface of their efforts, which include swaths of institutions, think tanks, and political activity groups they have founded or chiefly financed. The Kochs have largely subsidized the Institute for Justice, which opposes regulations in court; the Institute for Humane Studies, which underwrites libertarian academics; and the Bill of Rights Institute, which promotes a conservative slant on the Constitution.

By the time their efforts ramped up to full force, they were such a forceful presence in the beltway that officials within Obama's administration had to address their opposition actions, though perhaps not always directly. For the president's team is was important to emphasize that the Tea Party uprisings being cited in news reports were not an organic grassroots movement of the people, but a carefully cultivated astroturfing effort fostered by political operatives far removed from the everyday man and with a very specific and, in their minds, sinister agenda. "What they don't say is that, in part, this is a grassroots citizens' movement brought to you by a bunch of oil billionaires,"[13] said David Axelrod, Obama's senior adviser, in the aforementioned *New Yorker* article by Jane Mayer.

Eventually another group, Americans for Prosperity (AFP), would come about as an important link between the Kochs and the Tea Party.

"I've never been to a tea-party event. No one representing the tea party has ever even approached me," David Koch told Andrew Goldman in a 2010 piece that appeared in *New York* magazine.[14]

"To my knowledge, we have not been approached for support by any of the newer 'tea party' or other grassroots groups that have sprung up around the country in the past year or so,"[15] said Dr. Richard Fink, who at the time served as both a vice president for Koch Industries and the president of the Charles G. Koch Charitable Foundation, in an interview with Tim Mak of the *FrumForum*, the blog run by former George W. Bush speechwriter and senior editor at the *Atlantic* David Frum.

He would later in the same article deny the connection between AFP and the Tea Party, adding. "I don't consider them a Tea Party institution . . . [The group] has been active for nearly thirty years. While they participate in events with tea party groups, our support of them has included no funds specifically for tea party-related efforts."[16]

The 2010 documentary, *(Astro)Turf Wars* by Taki Oldham, tells a different story. The director finds his way into the 2009 Defending the American Dream Summit hosted by AFP and shows David Koch addressing the summit, saying "Five years ago my brother Charles and I provided the funds to start Americans for Prosperity. It's beyond my wildest dreams how AFP has grown into this enormous organization." Shortly after his keynote, local AFP organizers speak in front of Koch about how they set up local Tea Party events, and at no point does he deny a connection, but rather nods and smiles in seeming approval of the achievements. Eventually, the program breaks up into separate sessions to strategize future Tea Party events. Koch never mentions the group by name but at no point objects to the implication and display of close ties between an organization he founded and the Tea Party.[17]

Eventually, even the president alluded to skepticism over just who planted the grass on which the Tea Party marched. In a 2010 speech in Austin, Texas, President Obama opined: "Right now all around this country there are groups with harmless-sounding names like Americans for Prosperity, who are running millions of dollars of ads against Democratic candidates all across the country. And they don't have to say who exactly the Americans for Prosperity are. You don't know if it's a foreign-controlled corporation. You don't know if it's a big oil company, or a big bank."[18]

Along with calling out AFP by name, he bemoaned the *Citizens United* decision that was crucial to the expansion of the Kochs' mission as the 2010 elections approached:

> A Supreme Court decision allowed this to happen. And we tried to fix it, just by saying disclose what's going on, and making sure that foreign companies can't influence our elections. Seemed pretty straightforward. The other side said no . . . They don't want you to know who the Americans for Prosperity are, because they're thinking about the next election.[19]

That Supreme Court decision was crucial to the activities of the Kochs at the seminal moment for their movement, the 2010 election cycle.

Paul M. Secunda, associate professor of law at Marquette University, told the *Nation* in a 2011 feature by Mark Ames and Mike Elk that "before *Citizens United*, federal election law allowed a company like Koch Industries to talk to officers and shareholders about whom to vote for, but not to talk with employees about whom to vote for . . . Now, companies like Koch Industries are free to send out newsletters persuading their employees how to vote. They can even intimidate their employees into voting for their candidates."[20]

Emboldened by the Supreme Court decision, the brothers sent out a packet to fifty thousand employees with advice on who to vote for. A copy specifically tailored for employees in Washington state was obtained by the *Nation* in early 2011 and showed just how far the brothers efforts had gone, partly thanks to the freedom lent by the judicial branch. The packet even featured an editorial from Charles.

UCLA law professor Katherine Stone examined the election packet and was quoted in the story as saying: "Until *Citizens United*, this sort of political propaganda was probably not permitted. But after the *Citizens United* decision, I can imagine it'll be a lot more common, with restrictions on corporations now lifted."[21]

The paychecks for these organizations come with a price: deference to the donors. "If we're going to give a lot of money, we'll make darn sure they spend it in a way that goes along with our intent," David Koch said to Doherty, the editor of the Koch-owned magazine. "And if they make a wrong turn and start doing things we don't agree with, we withdraw funding."[22]

Just what comes in a deal with the Kochs is exemplified in a piece written by Kris Hundley in the *Tampa Bay Times* in 2011. In the piece, Hundley describes the situation where a foundation funded by the brothers pledged a $1.5 million donation to Florida State University, but in unorthodox fashion asked for the right to screen and sign off on new hires in exchange. As the piece detailed:

Traditionally, university donors have little official input into choosing the person who fills a chair they've funded. The power of university faculty and officials to choose professors without outside interference is considered a hallmark of academic freedom.

Under the agreement with the Charles G. Koch Charitable Foundation, however, faculty only retain the illusion of control. The contract specifies that an advisory committee appointed by Koch decides which candidates should be considered. The foundation can also withdraw its funding if it's not happy with the faculty's choice or if the hires don't meet 'objectives' set by Koch during annual evaluations.[23]

As George Monbiot described in a 2010 opinion piece in the *Guardian*, the connections between the Koch-funded groups and the Tea Party have existed since the start:

The movement began when CNBC's Rick Santelli called from the floor of the Chicago Mercantile Exchange for a bankers' revolt against the undeserving poor. (He proposed that the traders should hold a tea party to dump derivative securities in Lake Michigan to prevent Obama's plan to "[subsidize] the losers": by which he meant people whose mortgages had fallen into arrears.) On the same day, Americans for Prosperity set up a Tea Party Facebook page and started [organizing]Tea Party events.[24]

At an AFP-hosted event in 2004, chronicled in Mayer's *New Yorker* piece and hosted in Texas, event organizer Peggy Venable said the Kochs are "certainly our people. David's the chairman of our board. I've certainly met with them, and I'm very appreciative of what they do."[25] Venable is a proud Tea Party veteran and has been paid by AFP.

AFP was a middleman of sorts between the brothers and the "grassroots" movement. Days and weeks before the Tea Party Tax Day protests in April 2009, the AFP website offered up "Tea Party Talking Points."

The 2010 anti-government red wave elections were the result of the Kochs' efforts and their most tangible triumph in four decades as political operatives. After two years of fighting Obama's agenda, growing the Tea Party, and lobbing numerous attacks, they helped remove the Democratic majority. Midterm elections tend to skew conservative as voting is typically down, but libertarian and far right efforts made November 2, 2010 ring with anti-Obama sentiment.

In February of 2010, in a special election, the *Los Angeles Times* identified Long Island businessman Dean Murray as the first Tea Party candidate to win an election when he won a seat in the New York state assembly, serving as a harbinger of what would follow in November.

In the Senate, the Democratic majority was reduced from fifty-nine seats to fifty-three with the Grand Old Party (GOP) picking up six more seats out of thirty-seven contested. That was small potatoes compared to the bloodbath in the House of Representatives where Republicans picked up a whopping sixty-three seats to go from a 179-seat minority to a 242-seat majority. This was at least partially powered by the 138 candidates for Congress with support from the Tea Party as identified by the *New York Times*.[26] When all was said and done, *NBC News* reported that five candidates supported by the Tea Party took a seat in the Senate and forty in the House.[27] The Kochs' pet project now had its teeth in Congress and has ever since. Mission accomplished.

As described in the *New Yorker*,

The anti-government fervor infusing the 2010 elections represents a political triumph for the Kochs. By giving money to "educate," fund, and organize Tea Party protesters, they have helped turn their private agenda into a mass movement. Bruce Bartlett, a conservative econo-mist and a historian, who once worked at the National Center for Policy Analysis, a Dallas-based think tank that the Kochs fund, said, "The problem with the whole libertarian movement is that it's been all chiefs and no Indians. There haven't been any actual people, like vot-ers, who give a crap about it. So the problem for the Kochs has been trying to create a movement." With the emergence of the Tea Party, he said, "everyone suddenly sees that for the first time there are Indi-ans out there—people who can provide real ideological power." The Kochs, he said, are "trying to shape and control and channel the populist uprising into their own policies." A Republican campaign consultant who has done research on behalf of Charles and David Koch said of the Tea Party, "The Koch brothers gave the money that founded it. It's like they put the seeds in the ground. Then the rain-storm comes, and the frogs come out of the mud—and they're our candidates!"[28]

With increased exposure and coverage of their efforts beginning in 2010, the Kochs have fought back against the bad publicity, and have seemingly given up on recapturing the anonymity they enjoyed for their first three decades in politics.

As described in a Kenneth Vogel story that appeared in *Politico* in 2011, "They've hired a team of PR pros with experience working for top Repub-licans including Sarah Palin and Arnold Schwarzenegger to quietly engage reporters to try to shape their Koch coverage, and commissioned sophis-ticated polling to monitor any collateral damage to the image of their company, Koch Industries. At the same time, through their high-priced lawyers, private security detail and influential allies in conservative poli-tics and media, the Kochs have played hard ball with critics and sus-pected foes."[29]

The results of 2010 bore the fingerprints of the brothers' efforts from 2008 to 2010. It started just weeks after the presidential election when Charles Koch, in January 2009, cautioned in his company newsletter of the dire and unprecedented peril he saw in the state of the country and the recently elected progressive government. He characterized the country as facing the potential for an unparalleled loss of liberty and prosperity not seen since the 1930s, a decade ushered in by the Great Depression and ending with World War II.

AFP launched rallies against Obama's proposed stimulus spending, the Mercatus Center released a report that claimed stimulus funds were being given unfairly to Democratic districts and created the right-wing talking point of slush funds. Though it was eventually debunked and corrected, the damage had been done. An offshoot of AFP, Patients United Now organized an estimated three hundred rallies against healthcare reform along with "kill the bill" protests outside the capitol. Additionally, the top issue for the oil magnates was in the crosshairs as some eighty events were organized by AFP to combat legislation to expand cap and trade legislation, which limits the amount of pollution a company can account for but allows for companies to exchange their allowances, along with climate talks. In protests outside the United Nations Conference on Climate Change in Copenhagen, AFP president Tim Phillips described the movement against the climate talks as a "grassroots movement." The international talks yielded disappointing results for those wanting to see progress on global climate action.

There was little question that the efforts of the Tea Party, and its many arms and organizations tangential to the Kochs, were effective in hurting Obama and his agenda. Most importantly, it all looked like the grassroots will of voters, not the astroturf agenda of two rich brothers from Wichita, Kansas.

Grover Norquist, a conservative political advocate well known around the capital, spoke to Jane Mayer about the Republican leadership's stymieing of Obama's agenda despite a minority across the board in his first two years, saying it was only made possible by the Tea Party and their numerous protests, which started in August 2008. Norquist said "[we] couldn't have done it without August, when people went out on the streets. It discouraged deal-makers . . . When Obama was strong, the Chamber of Commerce said, 'We can work with the Obama Administration.' But that changed when thousands of people went into the street and 'terrorized' congressmen. August is what changed it. Now that Obama is weak, people are getting tough."[30]

David Koch came to Washington near the first anniversary of Obama's election and attended an AFP rally that tinged of success and triumph, feeling like a victory lap. This was out of character for the man who runs, in his own words, the largest company that you've never heard of. But these were unprecedented times for the Wichita native and he had had an unprecedentedly large impact on grinding the government to a halt and stopping a president he wanted so badly to see fail. Obama's poll numbers were taking a dive, the right was emboldened to oppose all his agendas, and the word "bipartisan" was anathema.

In the speech he made that day, as chronicled in the *New Yorker*, Koch exalted that "days like today bring to reality the vision of our board of directors when we started this organization, five years ago . . . We envisioned a mass movement, a state-based one, but national in scope, of hundreds of thousands of American citizens from all walks of life standing up and fighting for the economic freedoms that made our nation the most prosperous society in history. . . . Thankfully, the stirrings from California to Virginia, and from Texas to Michigan, show that more and more of our fellow-citizens are beginning to see the same truths as we do."[31]

He did not mention or discuss the Tea Party that day and has not done so much since. They prefer the shadows, they prefer to make it seem as if voters have somehow found the "same truths" because they are just that, truths, not because of a complex organized effort that was steadfast and mechanical in its spread of slanted information. The idea that two of the richest men on Earth and blue-collar folks from around the country would reach the same conclusions on government and policy was a better storyline and easier to sell. Who cared that it seemed implausible? It was too good a story not to be true.

The Kochs are far from anonymous in comparison to where they stood in 2008, but their work has been done: the Freedom Caucus holds seats and Obama had to push through compromised versions of the legislation he could have made happen with majorities he would never see again after 2010.

How these three decades of political activism came to birth a political movement, whether it was intentional, and why the brothers did not do this earlier all remain conjecture. As Ben Smith wrote in *Politico* in 2010: "The Kochs have long operated behind the scenes, though it was no secret that they underwrite much of the libertarian movement."[32] The facts of that assertion have not changed, but a wing of the libertarian movement, beneficiaries of the brothers' billions, has evolved into the Tea Party.

In the late eighties, the brothers found a piece of their business, Koch Oil, under investigation from the Senate Select Committee on Indian Affairs. The "Kochtopus" fought back with the help of the best lobbyists money could buy. Even after the grand jury investigation into the allegations had been dissolved, those on the Koch payroll continued to probe the committee staffers and their private lives. The Senate investigators were distressed by the methods. Kenneth Ballen, the counsel to the Senate committee, said of the efforts: "These people have amassed such unaccountable power!"[33]

CHAPTER 3
BROOKS BROTHERS AND MIAMI-DADE– THE 2000 RECOUNT

n the 2000 US presidential election, there were 105,372,669 votes cast for a total of ten candidates. The difference between the two front-runners winning the election, the only realistic competitors representing the Democratic and Republican parties, were the votes of a mere 537 Floridians, according to an Associated Press (AP) report published one year and five days after the historic election.

On December 13, 2000, Al Gore called George W. Bush to officially concede the election for the second time. He initially conceded on Election Day, November 7, 2000, but retracted when he found out just how neck and neck vote totals were in the Sunshine State, ushering in over a month of chaos. That night was full of surprises with the Associated Press Voter News Service calling the battleground state that would decide the fate of the executive branch for Gore early in the night and reversing to Bush later on, before settling on "too close to call," a precursor for the unprecedented uncertainty that would follow.

The circus began when national television networks followed AP's lead, based on early voting tallies and exit polling, calling Florida for Gore within an hour of polls closing in the majority of Florida that falls within the

Eastern time zone. This happened just before the Florida panhandle, with its central time zone and conservative politics, closed the polls. Vote totals in those reliably red counties pushed the vote counting services, and in turn the media that used them for their broadcasts, to change the state designation to "too close to call" before giving the state to Bush and, in another twist, then returning the state to the toss-up category. They would settle at night's end with Bush up by 1,784 votes and an automatic recount necessary under Florida state law. That initial machine recount took place over the three days following Election Day in the sixty-six counties that used machine ballots and was completed on November 10. With news that it lowered the difference separating the two candidates to nine hundred votes and the White House hanging in the balance, the eyes of the nation shifted southeast.

With the revelation that the vote totals were so close, both campaigns braced for what they assumed correctly would be a long and arduous process settled by legal experts and bipartisan governing bodies.

For obvious reasons, the historic result was subject to rigorous review in the days, weeks, months, and even years that followed. First came the aforementioned automatic machine recount as mandated under Florida Election Code 102.141. With both sides lawyered up and ready for a legal battle, the Gore campaign requested a manual recount in four counties, surpassing the minimum three precincts necessary to request a manual recount according to state law. For Broward, Palm Beach, Miami-Dade, and Volusia counties the campaign stuck on the losing end wanted disputed ballots to be counted by hand with their burden of proof to change the outcome.

The complications continued as the unprecedented event proved an insurmountable challenge for statutes usually reserved for local elections and thus paling in scope to the project being undertaken. On November 12, the recounts started and before long it was abundantly clear that the lawful deadline of November 14 was unrealistic. In order to extend that deadline, the Gore campaign, along with Palm Beach and Volusia counties, sued for deadline extensions.

Across the aisle the approach was exactly the opposite, Bush and company were happy maintaining the status quo. Despite the close calls and several twists and turns, they were the victor if nothing changed. It was Bush's election to lose.

Four days after the election, on November 11, as the automatic machine recount came to a close and the manual recount was looming, the Bush campaign, in conjunction with Florida voters, sued in federal district court seeking to stop all manual recounts through a preemptive injunction using the Fourteenth Amendment and semantics related to the way ballots were recorded in the state. The court ruled against them.

As the original deadline for recounts came and went, Bush clung on to what was a minuscule lead in the neighborhood of two hundred votes. A state judge, Florida's secretary of state, the Florida Supreme Court, Leon County Circuit Court, and both campaigns were involved in the building chaos as December approached with no certification of results or President-elect.

After recounts, suspensions, reinstatements, attempts at certification, stays, and appeals, the Florida Supreme Court unanimously ruled that the manual counts in Broward, Miami-Dade, and Palm Beach were required for certification and set November 26 as the earliest possible deadline to finally put an end to a national crisis.

When November came to a close, the Gore campaign was locked in a last-ditch effort to preserve their chances. Florida Secretary of State Katherine Harris had certified a Bush victory by 537 votes despite incomplete recounts in the contested counties. Gore's lawsuit to keep his chances alive and keep fighting for recounts was ruled against in two lower courts, but when it reached the Florida Supreme Court on December 8 the justices voted 4–3 in favor, rejecting the selective use of manual recounts in only four counties and turning their eyes to undervotes, ballots with no selection for president. Their decision ordered for all such votes to be manually recounted across the state.

With the hope for Gore to overturn the slimmest of loss margins dwindling and his window to turn the tides closing, the US Supreme Court would put an end to the mayhem and put a second member of the Bush family into the oval office. Contemporaneous to the jockeying down south, the Bush campaign had shifted their cause to be a two-front war, taking up a lawsuit that appealed its way to the highest court in the land. With the manual recount fought for and won by the Democratic candidate, Washington, DC, would supersede events in Florida.

On December 6, the Florida legislature, which was Republican-controlled at the time, held a special session aimed at appointing electors for the state that would pledge to Bush. This effort was within their rights according to the constitution but would be an unnecessary attempt to finalize an election being decided in the beltway. On December 12, the Florida House of Representatives would approve the measure to hand Bush the state's electoral votes, and in turn the election.

Contemporaneously, in a 5 to 4 vote on December 9, the US Supreme Court ruled in favor of Bush, stopping the latest recount mere hours after it had begun. Their ruling came down late on December 12 and detailed constitutional problems with the manner with which the recount was set to take place under state law. With the recount deadline coming only hours after the decision and the strict parameters laid out in that documentation, the ruling essentially put an end to the recount.

Despite vocally disagreeing with the ruling, Gore accepted it. The following day he conceded the election. George W. Bush became president-elect.

While the election officially ended, the controversy continued. In the hours before the Miami-Dade recount would be shut down, a strident group of activists descended upon the site of the recounts. At the time it seemed as if it was a group of concerned voters who felt that there should be light shed on some mixture of wrongdoing or unnecessary second-guessing. It was revealed later on that the majority of those who were causing a ruckus, pounding on doors, and screaming at recount poll workers were hired help, or astroturf. Protestors on site threatened to expose what they saw as malfeasance and expanded their ranks by bringing in locals with a similar viewpoint and agenda.

Just how riotous the demonstrations were is still debated and unclear, and those who support them say they were a simple exercise of First Amendment rights, namely freedom of speech and freedom to peacefully assemble. The recount was cancelled because the deadline for completion was unachievable, but the protests certainly played a hand in slowing things down for the three appointees chosen to handle the recount, Independents Myriam Lehr and David Leahy, as well as Democrat Lawrence King. As is important when trying to make a point through protest, these gatherings were in the view of the many national and local television news crews who were glued to those buildings, covering the biggest news story in the world at the time.

When all the smoke cleared, Democrats who had finished on the losing end of the most closely contested election in United States history would find numerous sources to blame: Gore's campaign for blowing an early polling lead; Gore for coming off condescending and impatient at debates; the United States Supreme Court for overruling the Florida State Supreme Court's decision in favor of Gore; Bill Clinton for leaving office in the wake of an impeachment scandal; Ralph Nader for running parallel to Gore on many issues and taking 2,882,955 national votes that likely could have given Gore not only Florida but also New Hampshire, nullifying Bush's ultimate five electoral vote victory; the Bush campaign for raising historic amounts of money; and campaign manager Karl Rove and vice presidential candidate Dick Cheney for using dirty campaign tactics first seen in the primary against John McCain.

Some of that blame was warranted and some was mere bitterness over a loss so close it was surely difficult to swallow. However, one piece of the equation was incomplete. Late in the game Rove and his team had pulled a trick that, to this day, remains largely unknown and may have had a potentially significant impact on the outcome. They designed a last-ditch effort to win, validating critiques of McCain who, after losing South Carolina to Bush in the primary, said, "I want the presidency in the best way, not the worst way."[1]

As alluded to earlier, the campaign rallied crowds to gather at the recount site in Florida as attempts were made to recount the democratic stronghold of Miami-Dade County. Those protesters at the time were viewed as a grassroots movement of concerned citizens looking to see Bush given the seat he deserved and to put the election mess behind the country. Eventually it would be called out for what it truly was, an astroturfing of Republican staffers clad in their stereotypical khakis and loafers paid to fly down south to cause a ruckus and to create a narrative that the country was ready to move on, regardless of whether more investigation was necessary. Once a light was shed on the true events of those tense days and weeks, that effort would become known, for obvious reasons, as the Brooks Brothers riot.

As could be expected, the riots involved principal figures of the Republican Party, including the infamous Roger Stone, a longtime confidant and noteworthy figure in the rise of President Donald Trump. Prior to helping put his longtime ally, Trump, in office, Stone's crowning achievement was his role in the 2000 riots. In the immediate aftermath of the riots, he did take ownership but disavowed accounts of other Republican operatives that linked him to the events, telling *CNN* at the time, "I was there as a volunteer. I knew nothing about the protesters other than the fact that I approve Republicans expressing their First Amendment rights."[2]

His sentiments would change years later, in telling fashion, serving as not only an admission of his role in the astroturfed riot but as an admission of just how integral the riots may have been.

"There have been many times I've regretted it," Stone told Benjamin Sarlin of the *Daily Beast* in 2008 as Bush's second term came to a close with a low approval rating. "When I look at those double-page *New York Times* spreads of all the individual pictures of people who have been killed [in Iraq], I got to think, 'Maybe there wouldn't have been a war if I hadn't gone to Miami-Dade. Maybe there hadn't have been, in my view, an unjustified war if Bush hadn't become president.' It's very disturbing to me."[3]

That article goes on to talk about the efforts of Stone as a mercenary and doesn't dance around the integral role he played in the riots:

> According to Stone, he didn't even want to get involved in the 2000 race at all until the GOP's recount head, James Baker III, called him up and asked him for his help. Stone said that Baker had helped him out in 1981 by getting Reagan and Bush to lend support to New Jersey Governor Tom Kean, whose campaign Stone ran. He owed him a favor.[4]

During a separate 2008 Florida election in which Stone was an adviser, his role in the 2000 rallies would be used in an attack ad. The Democratic candidate for Broward County Sheriff, Scott Israel, ran critical commercials against Republican incumbent Al Lamberti for his involvement with "the same Bush hatchet man who tried to steal the 2000 election." Nonetheless, as has been proven time and again, Stone is good at his job. Much like in 2000, Stone's man won the race.

It is clear the recounts were never about numbers for Stone and likely, by extension, Bush and the operatives who descended on that office. As Stone told the *Miami Herald* in 2008, "It's attack, attack, attack. Al Gore thought the recount was a high-minded policy debate. He didn't understand that it was an extension of a war, of a political campaign."[5]

Just days after the riots, Jon Lantigua wrote in *Salon*: "But the fact is that the fracas at Miami's recount headquarters was engineered and carried out by Republican Party operatives imported from the heartland, far from South Florida. Indeed, all on-the-scene reports coming out now indicate that the Miami protest was carried out by rent-a-rioters flown in by the Republican Party. GOP spokespeople have said that at least 750 Republican activists have been sent into South Florida from around the country to oppose the recount, with the party picking up the tab for a number of them. And last Wednesday, when a gaggle of protesters sprang into action in Miami, those efforts seem to have paid off."[6]

As is conventional wisdom among those who have looked back at those riots, Lantigua gives much credit for the recount stopping to the hired hands. He also cites an integral figure in the concerted efforts, Representative John Sweeney of upstate New York who was joined, according to the *Miami Herald*, by Senate Majority Leader staffer Elizabeth Ross and Thomas Pyle, an aide to the House Majority Whip.

The efforts featured all the major players as chronicled by London *Sunday Times* correspondent Tom Rhodes, who said he overheard talk of keeping campaign chief strategist and eventual Senior Advisor to the President Karl Rove abreast of the developments.

Two major catalysts for the unrest were pieces of news that hurt Republicans when they came to light. First, the three-person canvassing board opted for a recount of only contested ballots rather than a full recount with the Florida State Supreme Court deadline seeming ever more impossible to meet by the minute. The true spark plug was that same board opting to move to a smaller room closer to the scanning machines to expedite the process.

The latter, which occurred simultaneously with rumors of Gore picking up an additional 157 votes, led to the ringleader Sweeney ordering for his astroturf crowd to "shut it down" as reported by Paul Gigot in a *Wall Street Journal* column at the time.

It was only minutes later that roughly twenty-five people of those assembled began pounding on the doors and windows of the nineteenth floor tallying room echoing demands to, "stop the count, stop the fraud," according to the aforementioned *Salon* piece. Television cameras showed the events unravel.

Those who followed the orders of the ringleaders had earned their stripes in the Republican political machine. In a television report in 2008, *MSNBC* host Rachel Maddow said that at least a half dozen people, according to IRS records, received payment for their services from the "Bush-Cheney recount committee." Those conveniently in Miami at the time included: Tom Pyle, aide to Republican congressman Tom Delay; Garry Malphrus, former staff director of the House Judiciary Subcommittee on criminal justice; Rory Cooper, staff member with the National Republican Congressional Committee; Kevin Smith, former House Republican conference analyst; Stephen Brophy, former aide to Senator Fred Thompson; Matt Schlapp, Bush campaign staffer; Roger Morse, aide to Republican congressman Van Hilleary; Duane Gibson, aide to Republican congressman Don Young; Chuck Royal, aide to Republican congressman Jim Demint; and Layna McConkey, former assistant to Republican congressman Jim Ross Lightfoot.

In a *New York Observer* story published days after the unrest in South Florida, Joe Conason described the riot as a "brief but violent assault on the Miami-Dade County officials who were attempting to comply with the court's decision."[7]

Adding another nickname, the "bourgeois riot," he went on to decry the relative silence from the Bush campaign despite revelations that showed they were far from unconnected from the events:

Neither George W. Bush, the self-styled President-elect, nor any of his handlers and advisers, had a calming word to say in the wake of the disgrace done in their campaign's name. And why would they call for calm, when it was they and their allies on Capitol Hill who recruited, transported, fed, housed and directed the invasion of those "idealistic, enthusiastic young Republicans?" Subsequent newspaper reports have established that many members of the roving gang were in fact on the payroll of Republican members of Congress, including at least five dispatched from the office of House Majority Whip Tom DeLay.[8]

Conason goes on to detail reports that Bush and Cheney joked about the events over the phone during Thanksgiving dinner that year while celebrating the all but assured victory in the election.

The irony of Bush potentially speaking so openly about the riots is only compounded by the fact that he, while Governor of Texas, signed an election law providing for manual recounts of punch-card ballots that are dimpled and otherwise, something he and the astroturf individuals who descended on the Miami district vehemently opposed.

Sweeney proved to be at the center of it all. In a *New York Times* piece from November 2000, Dana Canedy and Dexter Filkins wrote, "Then before television cameras and angry Republican party supporters in front of the county building where the tabulation was being done, Representative John Sweeney, Republican of New York, said the board was influenced by the 'Democratic machine.' As protesters chanted and waved Bush/Cheney signs, Mr. Sweeney pointed over his shoulder and said 'thugs in that building are trying to hijack this election.'"[9]

Violent incidents were cited in many news reports, namely against Democratic Party chief Joe Geller and Democratic spokesman Luis Rosero. In the case of Geller, he was wrongfully accused of stealing a ballot, when in fact it was a sample ballot. He was promptly surrounded by the angry mob (accounts are mixed over whether things got physical). Demonstrators shoved Rosero into the midst of a news conference and he went on to tell the *New York Times*, "I was punched twice in the back and kicked once . . . Everyone needs to calm down and relax. I think we've hit a new low point here."[10]

That *Times* piece also sums up what happened after the riot, "Shortly after the angry demonstration subsided, the board convened and announced they had abandoned the recount."[11]

In a contemporaneous *TIME* magazine article, journalist Tim Padgett told the story of one such astroturf protestor: "Marjorie Strayer insisted she was just a Virginian on vacation in Miami . . . But Strayer, it turns out, is a top aide to New Mexico's Republican congresswoman, Heather Wilson, and was one of hundreds of paid GOP crusaders who descended on South Florida last Wednesday to protest the state's recounts. 'The system is unfair, inaccurate, fraught with human error!' Strayer cried. In a Winnebago outside, GOP operatives orchestrated the ranks up to the 19th floor, hoping to halt the tally of the largest potential lode of Gore votes. Republicans, not usually known for takin' it to the streets, got what they wanted. Just two hours after a near riot outside the counting room, the Miami-Dade canvassing board voted to shut down the count . . . What the world watched was a GOP melee."[12]

Beth Reinhard wrote about the events in the *Miami Herald* some eight years later, saying, "a political juggernaut was set in motion that helped quash a vote recount, and ultimately, change American history." The plan in those days, as described in the *Herald*, was highly orchestrated, including "eavesdropping on the Democratic recount team from a nearby trailer with a walkie-talkie."[13]

The optics of the event were paramount, and the mission was accomplished, but how much they had to do with the final outcome is unclear. But their guy, their horse in the race, would spend two terms as commander-in-chief. Republican representatives who had a hand in assembling the Brooks Brothers Riot claimed it was an integral measure in combating a potential flipping of the election results.

Even Gore and his running mate Joe Lieberman had a take on the events, saying in their complaint contesting the election:

Republican and other supporters of George Bush launched a campaign of personal attacks upon the Canvassing Board members and election personnel. . . . Some news reports described the protests as a "near riot." The *New York Times* . . . reported on November 24, 2000: "One non-partisan member of the board, David Leahy, the supervisor of elections, said after the vote [to halt the manual recount] that the protests were one factor that he had weighed in his decision."[14]

After the riots and the shut-down recount, controversy spread across the aisle to the Gore campaign as reports surfaced that the presidential candidate had spoken with Miami-Dade county Mayor and Democrat Alex Penelas. Accusations in several media reports said that Gore had tried get the recount back on track by using his connection to a local legislator in the same party who was mentioned during the vice-presidential search.

Much has been said about the events of November and early December 2000 in the years since it has entered the history books. From conspiracy theories to controversial allegations, the historic month where the country did not know who the next president would be were fodder. Among the reevaluations were extensive recounts and studies that, while obviously not intended to or capable of changing the outcome or rewriting history, solely looked to ask the question of just how, in a country with over a hundred million voters, did less than six hundred Floridians pick the next president. They also questioned whether those six weeks of uncertainty and legal battles between the campaigns had any realistic application. The essential question was how did Bush win, but perhaps more interestingly, is there any creative accounting that can be done in order to make Al Gore the forty-third United States president?

After the smoke cleared from the government's numerous conflicting and contemporaneous recounts, the matter was still high on the mind of a population wanting answers. The most pertinent reexaminations of the course of events, aside from the official government recounts, were commissioned by media.

First to the punch in reopening the controversy was an effort assembled by *USA Today*, the *Miami Herald*, and Knight Ridder. The three media companies called upon accounting firm BDO Seidman to take on four potential scenarios and only studied undervotes. Ballots were chosen for one of two reasons in most recounts, either falling into the classification of an undervote or overvote. Undervotes were ballots that did not make a choice for president while overvotes made more than one choice for president.

The study had to account for the way punch style voting works, with a punch card being inserted into a holder similar to a clipboard. With a specially designed utensil, voters punch holes for the designated candidates they choose. In that initial study they looked at four possible methods of tabulation: a lenient standard in which any alteration to a ballot counted as a vote; the Palm Beach standard in which a dimple counts as a vote if other races on the same ballot show dimples; the two-corner standard in which at least two corners of the ballot are removed; and the strict standard in which only fully punched votes counted. For the first three, Bush won by 1,665, 884, and 363, respectively. The final gave Gore the race, by an unbelievable double-take inducing three votes.

Following up on that original study, the same three organizations were joined by the *Tampa Tribune* and a handful of other newspapers in a full recount of all machine-rejected ballots, which encompassed overvotes and undervotes. In analyzing 60,647 undervotes and 111,261 overvotes for a total of 171,908 Floridian votes, they found Bush benefited by stricter standards and Gore by lower standards leading *USA Today*, who published the results, to say: "Who does it appear most voters intended to vote for? Answer: Gore."[15]

For that study the final tallies were Gore winning on both the lenient and Palm Beach standard by 332 and 242 votes, respectively, and Bush winning by the two-corner standard and strict standard by 407 and 152 votes, respectively.

Overvotes were necessary to any scenario leading to a Gore win, however, he never requested to have them done. That being said, there is evidence that Judge Terry Lewis, who oversaw the recounts as a circuit judge for Leon County Circuit Court, had intentions to do so.

Overvotes with write-in names were an under covered part of the disallowed vote count and Florida State University public policy professor and elections observer, Lance deHaven-Smith remarked on that in an interview:

> Everybody had thought that the chads were where all the bad ballots were, but it turned out that the ones that were the most decisive were write-in ballots where people would check Gore and write Gore in, and the machine kicked those out. There were 175,000 votes overall that were so-called "spoiled ballots." About two-thirds of the spoiled ballots were over-votes; many or most of them would have been write-in over-votes, where people had punched and written in a candidate's name. And nobody looked at this, not even the Florida Supreme Court in the last decision it made requiring a statewide recount. Nobody had thought about it except Judge Terry Lewis, who was overseeing the statewide recount when it was halted by the U.S. Supreme Court.
>
> The write-in over-votes have really not gotten much attention. Those votes are not ambiguous. When you see Gore picked and then Gore written in, there's not a question in your mind who this person was voting for. When you go through those, they're unambiguous: Bush got some of those votes, but they were overwhelmingly for Gore. For example, in an analysis of the 2.7 million votes that had been cast in Florida's eight largest counties, the *Washington Post* found that Gore's name was punched on 46,000 of the over-vote ballots . . . while Bush's name was marked on only 17,000.[16]

The largest recount effort was called for by the Florida Ballot Project. It was sponsored by the *Associated Press, CNN,* the *Wall Street Journal,* the *New York Times,* the *Washington Post,* the *St. Petersburg Times,* the *Palm Beach Post,* and Tribune Publishing, which included the *Los Angeles Times, South Florida Sun-Sentinel, Orlando Sentinel,* and *Chicago Tribune.* The National Opinion Research Center at the University of Chicago was chosen to conduct it. Their review was comprehensive and went through 175,010 ballots spanning not only the disputed districts and counties but the entire state. The total number of overvotes was 113,820 while there were 61,190 undervotes. Within the overvote category, 68,476 chose Gore and a minor candidate, while 23,591 chose Bush and a minor candidate but because those ballots made the voters intentions unclear they were not included in the final report.

The undervote and overvote totals amounted to a significant three percent portion of ballots, well beyond the difference between the two candidates when things were completed. The official count had been a 537-vote advantage for Bush, but in eight differing scenarios analyzed in this largest of recount studies, it was found that any other potential action or outcome would have favored Gore, with four of eight giving him the election and the other four further reducing the razor thin Bush margin.

As detailed in the final report, the Florida Supreme Court recount, which was ultimately overruled and took into account all undervotes from Palm Beach and Miami-Dade counties, would have reduced the difference to 154 votes.

Gore-winning scenarios were possible only under review of all uncounted votes across the state, a measure the campaign never actually asked for. If the statewide recount was done under the county custom standard, which allows for each county to tabulate based on the parameters of their individual county canvassing board and what they consider a vote for both overvotes and undervotes, Gore would have won by 171 votes with a total of 10,480 new votes in the mix.

If the statewide recount was done under the most restrictive of standards, there would have been an additional 5,332 votes counted with Gore prevailing by 115. On the opposite end of the spectrum, in the most inclusive of standards, the total votes added would have been 24,240 and Gore would have been victorious by 107 votes. Gore's last path to hypothetical victory came with the standard for a majority of counties, which would have added 7,811 new votes and the closest margin of the entire analysis with Gore taking it by a mere sixty votes.

In what is perhaps a knock on the Gore campaign, had the recount they had favored went through—it was initiated and never completed—Bush would have still been victorious, albeit by smaller margins ranging from 225 to 493 votes.

Using considerably less arithmetic, market research firm Harris Insights and Analytics held a nationwide poll from December 14 to 21, asking, "If everyone who tried to vote in Florida had their votes counted for the candidate who they thought they were voting for—with no misleading ballots and infallible voting machines—who do you think would have won the election, George W. Bush or Al Gore?"[17] Gore won that final, albeit pointless, poll 49 percent to 40 percent, with 11 percent uncertain or abstaining.

History has a knack for repeating itself. When protests erupted in response to the Affordable Care Act, White House spokesman Robert Gibbs used the events in Miami-Dade as an example of how he felt those protests were astroturfed.

As it was covered in the *Wall Street Journal*, "Mr. Gibbs compared the protesters with the 'Brooks Brothers Brigade' that he said appeared in Florida after the 2000 presidential election. 'I seem to see some commonality in who pops up at some of these things,' he said, without elaborating. 'You can see quite a bit of similarity between who shows up where.'"[18]

On Election Day in 2016, Hillary Clinton and Donald Trump traded leads in Florida throughout the night. At 8:18 p.m. Eastern Standard Time they actually found themselves virtually tied within 151 votes with 87 percent of the state reporting. For good measure, that is a staggering 3,977,181 votes for Clinton and 3,977,066 votes for Trump. The state continues to be a key battleground in choosing the commander-in-chief with Donald Trump winning the state on the way to the White House in 2016 and two races, for governor and senate, going to a recount in 2018.

Exactly how much the Brooks Brothers Riot impacted the larger picture of the 2000 US presidential election is unknowable. What is crystal clear fact is that 537 votes, two more than the member total for the entire Congress, ultimately made the difference between a Bush and Gore presidency, with four—if not eight—years of "what if," second guessing, and parallel timelines. The questions are endless. With this small of a margin there is seemingly an endless stream of factors that can be seen as game changing, factors that altered the very history of the world as well as the forty-third presidency of the United States. The potential scenarios and blame game has, in the almost two decades since, covered pretty much every angle. Most of these reexaminations or reproaches focus on what factor could, would, or should have altered the outcome. In the more than a year of campaigning, polling, reporting, canvassing, donating, debating, and opinion formulating that lead up to the election, what small tweak would have shook the fabric of our nation, and therefore changed the course of our civilization? The vast majority of nostalgia has focused on Election Day and before. What if they are looking in the wrong place? What if a handful of Republican staffers disguised as concerned citizens and used as astroturf for the sake of a result were successful in achieving their mission? Remember, that unique election could have been decided by even the smallest seemingly inconsequential actions. What if the "Brooks Brothers riot" got George W. Bush confirmed as the forty-third president of the United States of America?

CHAPTER 4
WAL-MARTING
ACROSS AMERICA
(SPONSORED BY WAL-MART)

S am Walton founded Wal-Mart in 1962, and seven years later, on October 31, 1969, he incorporated the company. As of January 31, 2017, the multinational retailing corporation consisting of superstores, discount stores, and grocery stores and headquartered in Bentonville, Arkansas owned 11,695 stores across twenty-eight countries under sixty-three different brand names.

It can be tough to know whether one is purchasing goods from the Walton family due to all the various banners, ranging from the original "Wal-Mart" in the United States and Canada, "Wal-Mart de México y Centroamérica" in Mexico and Central America, "Asda" in the United Kingdom, "Seiyu Group" in Japan, and "Best Price" in India; or the formidable in their own right retail warehouses of "Sam's Club" and other wholly owned subsidiaries in Argentina, Chile, Brazil, and Canada.

The largest company in the world by revenue, the *Fortune* Global 500 list in 2016 listed their earnings at $480 billion. They hold the title of largest employer with 2.3 million employees and they are also the largest grocery retailer in the United States (despite not solely selling groceries), as well as one of the most valuable companies by market value. Founder Sam Walton's heirs own more than 50 percent of the company through their holding company, Walton Enterprises, as well as individual holdings. Their nation of origin is the core of the business with 62.3 percent of sales coming from the United States in 2016. However, they have never been one to settle and as mentioned made successful investments in the United Kingdom, South America, and China along with unsuccessful investment attempts in South Korea and Germany.

First listed on the New York Stock Exchange in 1972, some sixteen years later, in 1988, they were the most profitable retailer in the nation, and again in 1989. This from a company limited to the South and Midwest as of the middle of that decade. In the early 1990s, they made their mark with a significant expansion from coast to coast with Sam's Club appearing in New Jersey in November 1989 and in Lancaster, California in July 1990. The flagship first appeared in the northeast in October 1990 when it opened up in York, Pennsylvania. For those following at home, that means a trader on the floor of the stock exchange couldn't feasibly drive to a Wal-Mart when they first started trading it and even after it reached the mantle of largest retailer by revenue.

Just how powerful and influential Wal-Mart truly is cannot be properly described with earnings statements, stock graphs, or market caps. A June 2009 study by researchers at several universities and led by the Tuck School of Business at Dartmouth College found that upon the opening of a Wal-Mart, median sales at similar high-volume stores drop 40 percent, at supermarkets they drop 17 percent, and at drugstores 6 percent. The Wal-Mart impact is so mind-boggling that a Loyola University Chicago study actually found a link between the distance from a store and the affect it has on a business. That direct correlation had the most impact in small towns.

Not only has academia explored the phenomenon that is the world's largest retailer, a National Bureau of Economics study in 2009 confirmed sizable negative effects for businesses competing with Wal-Mart and found five to ten miles from the newly opened big box stores.

This has been chief among the list of criticisms levied against the giant corporation, but that criticism has come from many directions—from labor unions and community groups to grassroots organizations and religious groups. They have even gotten their fair share of flak from environmentalists and their own employees and customers.

The economic impact has been the primary driving concern, but it has not been limited to such. They have faced claims of discrimination, unsavory product sourcing, unfair treatment of suppliers, poor working conditions and employee treatment, subpar environmental practices, abuse of public subsidies, and even slavery. The company has consistently denied wrongdoing and instead credited efficiency for their often unparalleled low prices.

Studies of the sheer magnitude of the company and some of the unwanted consequences of that power are endless. Some noteworthy findings include:

A 2001 study by McKinsey Global Institute found that Wal-Mart "directly and indirectly caused the bulk of the productivity acceleration"[1] in the retail sector.

The Economic Policy Institute found that for the decade-plus between 2001 and 2013 Wal-Mart had a trade deficit with China that accounted for 400,000 lost US jobs through the use of cheap labor in China.[2]

The University of Missouri found that a new location increases net retail employment in a county by one hundred jobs immediately, but within five years half of those disappear at retail competitors in the area, which often close.[3]

A 2004 paper from Pennsylvania State University found counties with Wal-Mart stores in the United States had greater rates of poverty than their non-Wal-Mart counterparts.[4]

A University of Melbourne lecture from September 2007 detailed a study in Nebraska that illuminated how Wal-Mart elicited changes within a town. A newly opened location was found to have barebones prices that beat out local competition, while a longer standing location in the same state had already "destroyed the local economy" and in turn had 17 percent higher prices.[5]

A 2005 article in the *Washington Post* said that, "Wal-Mart's discounting on food alone boosts the welfare of American shoppers by at least US $50 billion per year."[6]

In contrast to those damning claims, some have championed the free market prowess of the Walton family business. In a 2006 *Washington Post* column, George Will crowned Wal-Mart "the most prodigious job-creator in the history of the private sector in this galaxy,"[7] claiming that it creates two jobs for every one it eliminates at a competitor and comparing their savings for shoppers to the consumer help of food stamps and the earned income tax credit.

Similarly, a piece in the *Guardian* in 2004 highlighted the Wal-Mart Foundation, the corporation's philanthropic arm, and its efforts to boost its work with US manufacturers as well as a $10 billion pledge to support domestic manufacturing and plans to buy $250 billion in products made stateside over the decade following.

The ubiquity of Wal-Mart has even caused new words to be invented. "Wal-Marting" is a usually pejorative term, it can be in reference to globalization or the increased homogenization of retail businesses, or in a less negative connotation can refer simply to the practice of going shopping at the chain stores.

As a play on that term, a blog titled "Wal-Marting Across America" was started on September 27, 2006, by a couple named Laura and Jim. The folksy site was set up to chronicle the couple's maiden voyage in a recreational vehicle from Las Vegas to Georgia, parking in Wal-Mart parking lots wherever they chose to stop. As detailed in a Bloomberg News story by Pallavi Gogoi that appeared the month after the blog launched, the introductory post, written by Laura, said, "We are not bloggers, but since our lives have always been more journey than destination we are explorers at heart. . . . We figured we'd give it a go."[8]

Gogoi goes on to describe the tone of the blog and its disconnect with many accounts of the reality of being a Wal-Mart employee: "Every Wal-Mart employee that Laura and Jim run into, from store clerks to photogenic executives, absolutely loves to work at the store. Sound like a great Wal-Mart publicity campaign? Anyone familiar with Wal-Mart and its reputation for being quite stingy with wages and benefits will roll their eyes at such a rosy picture. In fact, some critics are so skeptical that they wonder whether Jim and Laura are real or whether they were concocted at the company's headquarters in Bentonville, Ark."[9]

That skepticism didn't take long to lead to questions. Jonathan Rees, a professor, labor historian, and former staff researcher at the American Federation of Labor and Congress of Industrial Organizations, posted on the website "The Writing on the Wal" openly challenging the concept that Laura and Jim were as advertised and asking for a reason for their motives and who supplied the funds for their transportation. His inclination, as he told Gogoi: "Wal-Mart has hired fake people."[10]

Wal-Mart's approach to doing business led to questions about how realistic these accounts were. How could a corporation that fought against a minimum wage increase in Chicago in 2010 and against a Maryland law requiring an increase in their health care spending also have handfuls of happy employees appearing conveniently on a serendipitously assembled blog?

Taking that question to its logical conclusion, was Wal-Marting Across America a company job? Are Laura and Jim, or at least the version we see of them, real? Was this a grassroots effort to show a cross-country journey that also happened to shed a positive light on a controversial corporation with questionable ethics? Or was it an astroturfed public relations campaign, a commercial masquerading as a wholesome, folksy blog?

The answer to those questions would turn out to be complicated. Jim and Laura were real; however, their story was far from as it seemed. When fully disclosed, namely with the consideration of certain intentionally obfuscated financial payments, the rosy picture showed that the grassroots were more astroturf.

The corporation's utterly desperate desire to find anyone willing to give a positive comment about their business is evident in the backstory of the blog. Far from the good graces of those supportive of moral business practices, when the blog first appeared Wal-Mart was in the cross hairs of politicians, union leaders, workers, and community groups challenging their employee treatment and business practices.

It is in the face of that criticism that Jim and Laura, fifty-eight and forty-two years old respectively, came into the picture. The unmarried couple had lived together for eight years in Washington, DC, and had three children between them. Both were forced to reveal their identities as more and more revelations came to light about the blog, which in reality was a public relations stunt cooked up by Wal-Mart.

Jim initially refused to reveal his last name or identity in defense of his employer, only saying he was a professional photographer (more on that later). His partner in their cross-country venture was Laura St. Claire. St. Claire was a freelance writer who worked with the United States Department of Treasury.

As St. Claire told it to Gogoi for her *Bloomberg Businessweek* story, though the ends were far from organic the beginnings were genuine. To hear St. Claire tell it, the couple happened upon a fleet of recreational vehicles in a Wal-Mart parking lot near the Grand Canyon. First thinking that perhaps some convention was in town, they later found out that the reason they had collected there was that the store allowed campers to park for free. They decided it would be a cost-effective way to visit their children at college in Pennsylvania and North Carolina. Additionally, she had designs on writing about the adventure in a publication geared toward RV owners and users.

Prior to setting off, they sought out permission from an organization supportive of the company, Working Families for Wal-Mart. The mention of that organization only further muddies the waters as it is advertised as an advocacy group formed by shoppers, but was actually created by the store's public relations firm, Edelman Public Relations. The group's creation was intended to counterbalance union-funded groups in opposition to the store, such as Wal-Mart Watch and Wake Up Wal-Mart.

Working Families for Wal-Mart was keen to the idea, even offering to sponsor the trip with certain tweaks. First and foremost, the trip would be supersized. The couple was flown to Vegas on the organization's dollar, there a mint-green RV was waiting for them featuring the Working Families for Wal-Mart logo. They would take that ride across the states to Georgia, and the venture was even given a name: Wal-Marting Across America. The name took a term previously used negatively and flipped it on its head.

St. Claire stands by the fact that their trip was planned before the group came along, but once they became involved, they came on strong. They took care of gas tabs, set up the blog and paid freelance fees for the posts Laura wrote. The connection is hard to miss, since Wal-Mart is admittedly the major benefactor for Working Families for Wal-Mart, though the specifics are unknown. With the gift of hindsight and the revelation that St. Claire was on the company dime, the blog is clearly more marketing than reporting. An example of this conflict in action can be seen from a post in Amarillo, Texas featuring a store employee (as many posts did):

Cragg Thompson joined the Wal-Mart team six years ago . . . Cragg's son, Brandon, contracted cardiomyopathy—a serious disease in which the heart muscle becomes inflamed and does not work as well as it should because of a viral infection. This necessitated expensive surgery and a pacemaker totaling over $300,000 in medical bills, paid for by Cragg's Wal-Mart Blue Cross Blue Shield Insurance. Today, 19-year-old Brandon Thompson has returned to work in the automotive department of the Pampa, Texas, Wal-Mart. Cragg feels his Wal-Mart's health insurance is a life saver . . . literally.[11]

Another example of that slanted commentary came from ground zero, the Bentonville headquarters where Laura wrote about Felicia Saenz in a post titled "From Cashier to Manager":

Now Felicia is a Project Manager for Corporate Strategy/Sustainability and is very proud of Wal-Mart's efforts to protect the environment. . . . Wal-Mart is working toward an energy use goal of 100% renewable resources; targeting zero waste from packaging by 2025 and selling products that are good for the world.[12]

When the site still existed it did feature a graphic for Working Families for Wal-Mart, but not any clear disclaimer of the corporate involvement in both the blog and advocacy group; furthermore, it made no mention that through those connections the corporation had funded the excursion and paid for the posts.

This effort was the tip of the iceberg in the Wal-Mart effort to improve their image through the best marketing money can buy. Working with Edelman, they looked to change the public perception by going beyond traditional avenues and using guerrilla marketing tactics as evidenced in Wal-Marting Across America.

Laura told *Businessweek* she didn't have the sense she was misleading anyone and even sounded like a company woman saying she found it "refreshing" that they hadn't encountered unhappy employees in their ventures. "We have not experienced one negative comment, and it's amazed us," she told Gogoi.[13] On Sunday, October 8, the couple arrived at their undisclosed destination in Georgia and on October 10, Laura posted her final post.

After the jig was up, having been exposed through reporting in *Bloomberg Businessweek*, Laura posted two final blog posts on October 12, 2006, at 5:19 and 7:52 a.m. The site featured posts within a teal letterbox framed by a thin white border backed by turquoise and a header featuring a map collage, the logo for the site that featured "Wal-Marting" in white stencil in an orange box and "Across America" diagonally in script below, along with a black-and-white picture of a vintage Chevrolet Corvette towing a trailer. To the left were sliders for different layouts including marine- and aviation-themed layouts. To the right it clearly designated the site was sponsored by Working Families for Wal-Mart and was clickable for anyone inclined to try or anyone looking for "the fine print," but it is safe to say it was still not particularly forthcoming that it was a marketing campaign. Who among us reads the fine print?

The penultimate post on the final day came at early dawn and was short and sweet. Titled "Thanks for Stopping, Bye," it talked about their arrival in Atlanta and lessons learned on the road, including "32-feet is nowhere near as big as it seems. Plus those doorways are the perfect height for a 6'2" person to bump his head (repeatedly)."[14] It goes on to tell of their time spent touring RVs at the Georgia National Fair with plans of an unspecified future "adventure." They chronicle stops at the meteor crater, Graceland, 16th Street Church, and Zuni Pueblo. The post goes through several conversations on the road and finishes with a note: "We want to send a special thank you to all the Wal-Mart associates and customers along the way that took the time to tell us their tales—whatever they may be."

Some two and a half hours later, the last post of the now defunct site would come along and be titled plainly "The Final Word." Also authored by

Laura, at least as far as the archived site says, it opens controversially by admitting fault: "Our blog was about the people we met and the stories they told. As a storyteller, I should have done a better job beginning at the beginning with our tale."[15]

From there, Laura goes on to describe the genesis of the project they had undertaken. It tells of how the couple first learned of Wal-Mart's parking lot policy in April 2006 while on a trip in the American Southwest. The post claims that in the early going they thought of the idea to see the country by renting an RV and taking advantage of free parking at the many Wal-Marts across the United States. This is where the aforementioned claims of an organic idea to chronicle the trip for hobby magazines is told, all leading to reaching out to Working Families for Wal-Mart for permission and the birth of their sponsored trip. She talks about the company's reaction when they posed the idea saying, "They didn't just give us permission. They said they would even sponsor the trip! A blog seemed the perfect medium to tell those stories—a perfect way to present a diary of my trip. I would post about the trip, not after the fact but from right out there on the road. And even more exciting, no editors! What writer could say no to that?"

Laura, in her confessional post, describes the partnership between the couple and Working Families for Wal-Mart as a "perfect fit" before admitting that was not a consensus opinion.

"Not everybody saw it that way, though. While we were on the road, a blogger asked if we were real people. We are. We're real people, and we took a real RV on a real trip and wrote real stories about it. And the people we met, many of whom I wrote about on the blog, are all real people too. Not paid spokesmen. Just real people, all of whom gave us permission to tell their stories."

Laura was referring to voracious skepticism and opposition to the trip, which led to the revelation of the sponsorship and would ultimately reveal

Jim to be an employee of the *Washington Post*. (More on that later!) The author refers to the "organized Wal-Mart opposition group" and condemns those responsible. "We had heard that Wal-Mart's critics could be vicious in their attacks. Now we know those concerns were valid."

After the revelations came stern condemnation from those against the retailer, and, in her parting words, Laura addresses that by saying the opposition groups can't deny their words just because they solely found people with positive stories:

> I've met too many people—real people, not imaginary Internet people—who've told me about all the good Wal-Mart has done. I've camped in Wal-Mart parking lots. I've met these people and heard their stories firsthand. Which is something the people who attacked Jim and me haven't done and don't care to do.
>
> So I've made the trip. I had a great time. I loved meeting the people we met, listening to the stories we heard. After everything that's happened, I even loved blogging about it all. And if I had the chance, I'd do it again. In the end, that's all that really matters.

Among the dissidents who exposed the astroturf marketing campaign, forced the hand of Laura to include that tell-all post before closing up shop, and championed the revelations of their true identities were other blogs, including the aforementioned Writing on The Wal in which writer Jim Rees responded step-by-step to the campaign, making his own posts that featured skepticism turned dissatisfaction upon the confirmation that Wal-Mart was involved and the grassroots effort wasn't as it seemed.

A noteworthy day of posts came from Rees on October 3 in which his writing of two open letters to the bloggers even elicited a direct response at a time when the nature of the project was still unclear. In the first of two open letters, Rees is fairly blunt: "Please prove to me that you exist."[16] Acknowledging that he is being rather callous, he goes on to ask the couple if they realize that the blog sponsor, plainly advertised on the side panel and through which he found the site, was sponsored by Wal-Mart and Edelman Public Relations. He points out the odd fact that there are no comments on "Wal-Marting Across America," but then takes the track of unawareness as to whether the tour guides were in on the rouse or simply ignorant to the orchestrators.

He goes on to detail that his initial demand was partially for effect but also somewhat literal as marketing firms have invented people in the past. He asks for more information on the couple by using the little he has been told:

> For example, Laura tells us that she is 42 years old with no kids at home. Do you have a job, Laura? Does Jim? You see, according to John Tierney writing in the *New York Times*, "The average Wal-Mart customer has an income of $35,000." I'm thinking you can't afford to buy an r.v. and drive across America unless you make a lot more than that. And what about those lost earnings from your trip? If you do exist, how much is Edelman paying you to do this?[17]

He goes on to offer to post their response on the blog. The couple did respond but through private email and though that correspondence never came to light, just seven hours later Rees took to his site to chronicle the exchange and more.

In the follow-up, there is not much that is made clearer and it seems that the stars of "Wal-Marting Across America" did not reveal all the details but did at least feel obliged to admit they were living, breathing humans. Rees mostly asks follow-up questions to which he never gets a direct answer, but all is laid out in the aforementioned ultimate piece the blog posted. He says in the closing of "Another Open Letter to 'Jim' and 'Laura'":

> I get the impression that you two are trying to have it both ways. Either way, don't you think people who read your blog deserve to know exactly what your relationship with Edelman and Wal-Mart is so that they can judge for themselves whether you are a credible source for information about the company? Let's start with an easy one: Who's paying your gas bills? If yours is anything like the RVs I've seen on the road, that's gotta be a big chunk of change. I eagerly await more proof that you are not props of the Edelman/Wal-Mart propaganda machine.[18]

By the time the truth came out, it would be a bigger story well beyond the two counteracting blogs. Wal-Mart Watch revealed that Jim was in fact a photographer for the *Washington Post* named James Thresher and *Bloomberg Businessweek* said, "Wal-Mart is paying plenty for their support."[19]

In October of 2006, Jim's employer, through staff writer Howard Kurtz, addressed the *Post*'s reaction to the revelation which, regardless of their stance on the store chain, was far from an ideal situation for the newspaper to be involved in.

Kurtz discussed the clear conflicts involved in the work, including the fact that Working Families put out a press release for the start of Thresher and St. Claire's adventure in which they quoted Interim Chairman of Wal-Mart Catherine Smith who said, "America's working families benefit from Wal-Mart . . . We wanted to take that a step further so two of our members are hitting the road to hear, first hand, the many opportunities Wal-Mart provides to its customers and associates."[20]

The executive editor at the time, Leonard Downie Jr., viewed the online travelogue as a violation of the *Post*'s outside work policy. *Businessweek* ran with the story and Thresher eventually agreed to repay Working Families for Wal-Mart some $2,200 for his share of the trip expenses, reimbursing the advocacy group connected to the superstore for their airfare, RV, gas, and food from the ten-day journey.

The story quoted Thresher as saying, "Maybe it's something I shouldn't have done, in hindsight, obviously, but I didn't think I was out there compromising the *Washington Post*. It really seemed harmless."[21]

It also quoted his employer, Downie, as saying, "We do not allow our staff to freelance for competitors, governments or special-interest groups. I regard Working Families for Wal-Mart as a special-interest group. . . . We are covering the debate going on over Wal-Mart's locations, business practices, et cetera. We can't work for one side or another in a public debate."[22]

Thresher, who had spent twenty-five years with the paper, had spoken with his superior, Assistant Managing Editor Joe Elbert, for permission to take on an assignment that involved Wal-Mart; however, the connection with the Working Families organization was not disclosed.

"I just got bushwhacked," Elbert said in the *Post* piece. "I feel terrible about it." In the same story he also referred to Thresher as a "wonderful photographer" before adding that "he probably didn't seriously consider the repercussions, and I didn't look into it enough."[23]

Thresher insisted he had done the right thing in the way he brought things up the chain. His partner had also done work for the *Post*, logging more than seventy restaurant reviews.

Edelman Public Relations was equally involved in the astroturf campaign and claimed the trip was designed "to capture Wal-Mart stories," and admitted to knowing Thresher's profession.

The level of financial support from the support group was unclear. Ultimately, Thresher defended his project in the paper he worked for: "Thresher defended the trip, saying that 'everything we wrote on that blog was true' and that Wal-Mart opponents had 'outed' him in an attempt to embarrass the company. 'I really didn't think anybody would know who I was,' he said. 'I was sort of nameless and faceless in all this.'"[24] As a result, amendments were made to the *Washington Post*'s policies.

Prior to the blogs, Edelman Public Relations was anonymous. Unlike Wal-Mart, there was not baked-in vitriol against the major company prior to the launch and subsequent shuttering of "Wal-Marting Across America." On October 20, 2006, MediaShift, a site dedicated to media and technology, highlighted that the public relations firm was behind the blog and two other pro-Wal-Mart sites, and was not exactly transparent about their efforts. Edelman promptly apologized for their involvement after an admission of guilt. "Edelman admits there are two other blogs it has surreptitiously run as 'flogs' or fake blogs,"[25] said the story by MediaShift founder Mark Glaser.

It turned out Edelman was also behind Working Families for Wal-Mart, which helped launch Jim and Laura's breakout site as well as a site called "Paid Critics." This pushback led to greater calls for transparency and a revelation that what once appeared as grassroots now was known to be astroturfing. As detailed by CNN Money:

Before Thursday, the authors of the blogs were not disclosed. But Web critics had been skeptical of claims that the blogs were grass-roots efforts, and pushed for greater transparency. In response to comments and emails, we've added author bylines to blog posts here at forwalmart.com, said a recent post to the site. Recent entries on Working Families for Wal-Mart are now attributed to "Miranda," and a click reveals that this is Miranda Gill, an Edelman employee. Recent entries on Paid Critics, a site dedicated to drawing links between Wal-Mart critics and groups, such as unions, with vested interests are written by Brian and Kate. These are Edelman employees Brian McNeill and Kate Marshall.[26]

The controversy caused a response that spread from anti-Wal-Mart groups primed with pitchforks and quickly moved to a mass audience. It led to an apology from Richard Edelman, president and CEO of Edelman Public Relations. The term "flog" was popularized as a result, both a shortened version of "fake blog" and a criticism of the dishonest effort.

Apologetic sentiments from Edelman's blog included: "Let me reiterate our support for the WOMMA (Word of Mouth Marketing Association) guidelines on transparency, which we helped to write. Our commitment is to openness and engagement because trust is not negotiable,"[27] were met with unapologetic rebuttals such as "Apparently for Edelman, transparency is just another pretty face,"[28] from *Consumer Reports* subsidiary, *Consumerist*. On the same site, they joked that flogs didn't fully cover it, and that they should be called "clogs" for "commercial blogs," adding, "Corporations are trying to leverage the same dubious media tactics on the internet they've used to subvert the so-called popular press. With the power of horde-based fact-checking, at least now we can unmask them quicker."[29]

WOMMA maintains six key guidelines around consumer protection and honesty. As spelled out in the aforementioned piece in *Bloomberg Businessweek* by Pallavi Gogoi from October 2006, "Outsiders marvel that the firm could go so far off track." The same piece quoted lawyer-turned-blogger Kevin O'Keefe, who founded LexBlog and helps law firms set up their own blogs, as saying, "They certainly weren't doing what they preached."[30]

The *Guardian* offered similar sentiments, saying, "All this seems more than a bit naive, and it's hard to believe the entries would have been so (in Business Week's phrase) 'relentlessly upbeat' if they weren't being paid for."[31]

"So, where was the problem? Not once, anywhere, was the fact that this was a PR stunt, with paid bloggers, disclosed. Readers were lead (sic) to believe that the tour had no relation to Wal-Mart and it was just two people who decided to start to make a blog about their experiences. Once the secret was out, this story blew up the PR world," said Kiley Skene in a piece on the events that ran in *News Generation* years later in April 2014. The site is representative of a media relations company and ran the story as a case study in poor public relations. "It is unfortunate that Edelman, the PR company working with Working Families of Wal-Mart at the time, did not realize that this same idea may have worked successfully if they had announced it as a public relations campaign and not something put on by an independent media outlet. Although the rules for blogging are not as set in stone as those in different kinds of media, especially in 2006 when blogging was much newer than it is now, this use of deceptive techniques doesn't do anything to win over consumers."[32]

Jim and Laura, as well as Working Families for Wal-Mart and Edelman Public Relations, were on the frontline of the ire, but Wal-Mart itself remained the reason the blog was viewed with such negative sentiment. The superstore chain kept itself as distant as possible, seemingly maintaining whatever space they could.

"We won't comment on the RV tour, since it was a Working Families for Wal-Mart initiative and we didn't have anything to do with it,"[33] Wal-Mart spokesman David Tovar told *Bloomberg Businessweek*.

That same piece continued to bash Edelman and specifically the company's CEO and namesake by saying "The question in the blogosphere is: How could Edelman have tried to pull something like this over on us? After all, Richard Edelman has lectured blog writers, America's largest companies, and even politicians on how to use this new medium."

Along with Edelman, blogging expert Steve Rubel was also among the suspected architects of the effort. Duncan Riley, a recognized blogger at the time, wrote an open letter to Rubel saying: "Your employer, Edelman, is embroiled in a pretty shady astroturfing scandal. A fake blog promoting Wal-Mart," and went on to ask for his response.[34]

Another critique came from communications specialist Shel Holtz that October when she opined, "So where is Edelman in this particular conversation? Missing in action."[35]

As Edelman began to feel the wrath that many were already pointing at Wal-Mart, he finally responded in time: "I want to acknowledge our error in failing to be transparent about the identity of the two bloggers from the outset. This is 100% our responsibility and our error; not the client's." Rubel added: "Our firm failed to be completely transparent. I am sorry I could not speak about this sooner. I had no personal role in this project."[36]

Nielsen Buzzmetrics Chief Marketing Officer Pete Blackshaw told *Ad Age* of the fallout that, "on the surface, they are contrite, apologetic and embarrassed, as anyone in the PR business is going to be embarrassed by their own PR crisis. The question is: To what extent is this incident going to help them take positive steps toward change?"[37]

Blogger and author Steve Taylor opined: "And so, what, we're supposed to say, 'Okay, Richard, all is good in Edelman-land again?' If you were newbies just getting your proverbial feet wet in the blogosphere, that'd be one thing, but for your agency, one that prides itself on being plugged in to the Web 2.0/social-media world, to have made this sort of crass mistake is a bit shocking."[38]

CHAPTER 5

MICROSOFT FOR TECHNOLOGY LEADERSHIP

I n 2016, Microsoft Corporation was the largest software maker by revenue according to *Forbes*, and among the world's most valuable companies.

The Redmond, Washington–based outfit was founded in 1975 by Bill Gates and Paul Allen who, thanks to the company, currently stand as the second and twenty-first richest persons in America, respectively. Their rise to dominance began with developing and selling BASIC interpreters for the Altair 8800, an interpreter for an early computer programming language, but would hit notable landmarks with the creation of the MS-DOS operating system in the mid-1980s, followed by the still running, constantly-in-development Microsoft Windows operating system.

In 1986, their initial public offering cemented their elite status as a multi-national technological corporation and created three billionaires and twelve thousand millionaires within their ranks. Today they continue to be a force to be reckoned with within the sector, adding to their portfolio with LinkedIn and Skype, which they purchased for $26.2 and $8.5 billion, respectively.

Those two entities are among the several subsidiaries within the corporation, which include internet search engine Bing, video game system Xbox, digital services market MSN, mixed reality developer HoloLens, cloud computing system Azure, and software development group Visual Studio.

Another component of the company, unbeknownst to many at the time it was set up, was Americans for Technology Leadership. This coalition of technology companies, organizations, and professionals were in the business of advocacy. Their cause was lobbying for stricter limitations for government regulation within the technological sector. The problem with that is that, while they tried to be seen as a grassroots organization, they came to be known and recognized as a front organization for the whims of their beneficiaries, first and foremost Microsoft.

This revelation would come to light in 2001 when, in the face of a United States antitrust law case, the company was found to be behind a campaign to deceive newspapers into believing large swaths of people were siding with Microsoft in the case and were thus unhappy with the actions against the private sector by the United States Department of Justice (DOJ).

United States v. Microsoft Corporation, the case that attempted to check the power of the tech conglomerate, accused them of anticompetitive practices ultimately leading to a monopoly in violation of the Sherman Antitrust Act of 1890 and more specifically the first two sections of the law. On May 18, 1998, the DOJ and twenty states, along with lead prosecutor Joel I. Klein, initiated the case.

The allegations held that Microsoft was abusive and monopolistic in the Intel-based personal computer industry stemming from their use and proliferation of their operating system and web browser sales. At issue was whether the company could bundle Internet Explorer with their operating system, a move that ultimately led to the abundance of its popularity with every Windows user inheriting the browser and thus restricting the abilities of competitors. Additionally at issue were suspicions that the company manipulated its interface to favor its own web browser software. This came along with a licensing agreement with equipment manufacturers and all the aforementioned conflicts leading to questions of the company's intent in bundling the software.

The company's argument was that the connection between their two popular products was a result of innovation and competition with the products being of a piece. The contrarian stance was that the two were separate products with no need to be tied together, as evidenced by the availability of Internet Explorer on the Macintosh Operating System. Those opposed to Microsoft also challenged the assertion that Internet Explorer was free with Windows because the costs of its upkeep likely drove up the bundled price.

Interest in the company from the US government did not come overnight. In 1992, the Federal Trade Commission (FTC) submitted an inquiry about whether Microsoft was functioning as a monopoly with the use of its massively popular personal computer operating system. In that instance, FTC commissioners were left hanging with a 2–2 vote the following year in 1993, leading to the closure of the investigation. However, soon thereafter, on August 21, 1994, Attorney General Janet Reno and the DOJ opened a separate investigation. Reno's investigation was settled in July 1994 with the company agreeing not to tie other products to Windows sales but maintaining the freedom to add features to the system. That became the precedent on which the debate over whether Internet Explorer was a feature of Windows or a separate product began.

Microsoft was sued by the DOJ and twenty state attorneys general for illegally stagnating competition in a move to protect and extend a monopoly on software. The trial began on May 18, 1998, and another suit was brought subsequently by the DOJ in October 1998 alleging that Microsoft violated the 1994 agreement by making manufacturers include Internet Explorer as part of Windows.

The case found on November 5, 1999, that Microsoft's dominance in the market of personal computer operating systems at the time constituted a monopoly, a problem only exacerbated by efforts to destroy threats in the space. That finding concluded that Microsoft was in violation of Sections 1 and 2 of the Sherman Antitrust Act in attempting and committing monopolization. Microsoft appealed the decision immediately. That original judgment also called for the company to be broken up into two independent units to produce the operating system and software.

An appeal was turned down by the United States Supreme Court and instead landed in federal appeals court. The DC Circuit Court of Appeals overturned the original ruling against Microsoft in part because of the scope of liability with which the remedies were ordered as well as questionable behavior on the part of the original judge, Thomas Penfield Jackson.

Jackson concluded that Microsoft had violated antitrust laws and ultimately requested a remedy proposal from the DOJ and attorneys general.

The DOJ announced on September 6, 2001, that they were no longer looking to break up Microsoft but simply to pursue a less severe penalty under the antitrust provision. In response, Microsoft drafted a proposal to settle under the condition that they allow personal computer manufacturers to integrate non-Microsoft software.

The Microsoft settlement proposal was drawn up by the company in advance of more talks with the government with the aim of closing the case. It came in the wake of failures on prior settlement efforts and with the government in turn drafting rules and restrictions for the court to impose in lieu of the company break-up that was out the window after the decision by the appellate court. The restrictions would go on to be debated and heard before US District Judge Colleen Kollar-Kotelly. The government was looking for rules that enabled computer makers to choose other software offerings instead of being forced to use Microsoft-licensed choices. There were also expectations that the government would look to single out competitor products that were a threat to Microsoft's monopoly. Microsoft was expected to fight the rumored restrictions.

Two years prior, Microsoft had offered a proposal to end a handful of contract and licensing provisions, increase disclosure of company practices, and open their desktop to more competitors. Those settlements were deemed inadequate.

"It is imperative that Microsoft not have another opportunity to use Windows XP to suppress competition in emerging Internet areas,"[1] said a statement by New York Attorney General Eliot Spitzer and California Attorney General Bill Lockyer.

"We look forward to continuing to work with the Department of Justice in the proceedings that are about to begin before the trial court, but will, if necessary to protect the public, press for remedies that go beyond those requested by the department," Spitzer and Lockyer added.[2] A piece in the *Wall Street Journal* in September 2001 by John Wilke quoted Richard Blumenthal, Connecticut's attorney general, as saying, "There will have to be active oversight of compliance . . . Enforcement has proved to be the quicksand for past conduct-based remedies."[3]

In the midst of settling this case, Microsoft faced an expanding investigation in Europe, as well as potential lawsuits from other companies. The general counsel for rival tech company Sun Microsystems, Mike Morris, said to the *Wall Street Journal* that "we are evaluating that carefully, on behalf of our shareholders, our customers and the industry . . . we'd be remiss in our fiduciary responsibility if we didn't take a hard look at a private antitrust action."[4]

The rollout of Windows XP was scheduled for fall 2001 and looked likely to be exempt from the ruling based on the tight timeline. Iowa Attorney General Tom Miller told *WSJ*, "When the judge enters a decree, it will be forward-looking and apply to all of Microsoft's products, including Windows XP," he said. "If XP is out of compliance, Microsoft would have to bring it into compliance as soon as possible."[5]

At the time, XP featured potentially problematic connections with the company's internet browser, media player, and instant-messaging software, along with a new e-commerce service.

"The issue isn't simply whether or not [Microsoft] is extending Windows, but how that stuff gets packaged and sold," Drew Brosseau, an analyst with SG Cowen, told the *Journal*.[6]

On November 2, 2001, the two sides settled the case under the agreement that Microsoft would share interfaces for application programming with third-party companies with the subsequent creation of a three-person panel with full access to the company system, source code, and records for five years for compliance assurance. Microsoft received a preferential result in comparison to the original ruling as they were able to maintain their code and tie their software in with Windows going forward.

In August of 2002, the company announced concessions they would make to fulfill the settlement and, in November of that same year, the judge accepted the terms. Nine of the twenty states that brought the suit, along with the District of Columbia, were against the terms under the premise that they believed it was not stringent enough to curb anticompetitive measures taken by Microsoft.

At the top of the corporate ladder for the tech giant was William H. Gates III, the founder of Microsoft and the second richest man on Earth (Jeff Bezos, founder of Amazon, is currently the richest, though his upcoming divorce could change that). His role in the events leading up to the case was chronicled with increased specificity and scrutiny in a piece that appeared in *Bloomberg Businessweek* in November 1998. Discussing how Gates fit into the stern allegations, the story said, "The allegations paint a picture of a modern-day robber baron. Like most high-profile trials, the antitrust extravaganza starring Bill Gates is being played out in two courts: the court of law and the court of public opinion . . . the Bill Gates aura is so far undamaged."[7]

Today, Gates's legacy is the stuff of legend. From dropping out of Harvard University at age twenty to founding a historically large software company and amassing a fortune that makes him among the richest individuals in history, he has amassed a cultlike following and has been called a visionary genius, complete with the speaking engagements that come with that kind of admiration. The self-made billionaire's book *The Road Ahead* was a bestseller in 1996.

The antitrust case was far from ideal for the Gates brand. In videotaped testimonials, he was described by the media as argumentative and his mannerisms and answers framed as "squirms and hedges," according to the aforementioned Bloomberg piece, adding that "many of the technology chief's denials and pleas of ignorance have been directly refuted by prosecutors with snippets of e-mail Gates both sent and received."[8]

A poll conducted by *Businessweek* and Harris Polling at the time found that he was still admired by 32 percent of respondents, while that number had been 37 percent prior to the trial and the 8 percent who did not like him was stagnant regardless of the legal proceedings. This may have had to do with the fact that the media coverage did not garner much public interest, as the same poll found that 54 percent were unaware of his testimony. Of those who heard the testimony and were aware of the trial, half held a favorable view of his approach. Though the company felt it necessary to lobby by any means necessary for their perception of the events, Gates was not in need of the same public relations, as 47 percent of people thought the government was unfairly hindering Gates as opposed to only 34 percent feeling he was too powerful. "There are plenty of businesspeople out there quietly cheering: 'Go, Bill, go,'" said Edward Segal, an expert in crisis communications in Washington, DC, to Bloomberg. "He's standing up to the government."[9]

"People are more interested in our products than they are in our legal briefs," added Chief Operating Officer Bob Herbold in the Bloomberg article. Nevertheless Gates did make rounds of public appearances at the time in a somewhat transparent and obvious attempt to tell his side of the story and cultivate some positive marketing.

"This case will say a lot about who our heroes are," mused W. Michael Hoffman, executive director of Bentley College's Center for Business Ethics, to Bloomberg.[10]

In the thick of the case, Microsoft battled the allegations both in the courtroom and in the public arena. Their public relations claim was that attempts to innovate within the sector were being stymied and attacked by companies that were both jealous and direct rivals. They asserted that the government actions were merely a front for the whims of their competitors. The Independent Institute, a California think-tank, ran full-page ads in the *New York Times* and the *Washington Post* on June 2, 1999, featuring "An Open Letter to President Clinton from 240 Economists on Antitrust Protection." It said:

> Consumers did not ask for these antitrust actions—rival business firms did. Consumers of high technology have enjoyed falling prices, expanding outputs, and a breathtaking array of new products and innovations. High technology markets are among the most dynamic and competitive in the world, and it is a tribute to open markets and entrepreneurial genius that American firms lead in so many of these industries. But, these same developments place heavy pressures on rival businesses, which must keep pace or lose their competitive races. Rivals can legitimately respond by improving their own products or by lowering prices. Increasingly, however, some firms have sought to handicap their rivals' races by turning to the government for protection. Many of these cases are based on speculation about some vaguely specified consumer harm in some unspecified future, and many of the proposed interventions will weaken successful U.S. firms and impede their competitiveness abroad.

With public opinion being a factor as always, and even more so with attorneys general in an election year, polling was problematic for those in the government looking to be harsh with the company. Of those polled, 67 percent said the antitrust suit was a waste of taxpayer dollars, 55 percent said Microsoft was a benefit to customers, 80 percent thought the case should be settled out of court, and 16 percent said they should break up the company. *USA Today* summarized the findings of the poll as saying that the case was a waste of money.

Consequently, that poll was conducted on behalf of, you guessed it, Americans for Technology Leadership. The group gets money from Microsoft, but how much is unclear. They were founded in 1999 as an offshoot of another company friendly group, Association for Competitive Technology.

This revelation led to a *Slate* story in March 2000 in which the reporter looked for the root of that study and group:

I had never heard of Americans for Technology Leadership, and a search on Yahoo led me to an October 29, 1999, press release announcing the organization's debut. The release said Americans for Technology Leadership was 'a new grassroots coalition.' It also cited an earlier poll 'presented by' the coalition, which found that '63 percent of Americans familiar with the DOJ suit against Microsoft believe the government should not be pursuing the case and 77 percent feel that it is an example of wasteful government spending.'

There was also a link to the group's home page. On the homepage was a link to a list of the group's founders. And if you haven't already guessed, there on the list of founders of the 'grassroots' organization, is the Microsoft Corporation.[11]

A contemporaneous story for CNET looked closer at the seemingly bogus polls. Mason Dixon Polling and Research had conducted the study as prompted by Americans for Technology Leadership and the Association of Competitive Technology.

It is clear now, and was starting to become clear then, that those two groups were in the pockets of Gates and Microsoft. The study would take place from Jan. 20 to 23 and poll a total of 1,124 registered voters with relative balance across the political spectrum. It was an effort to influence public policy and help in the face of the antitrust battle. Though it was the first to the table, the CNET story voiced a commonly held thought that the public relations battle was far from over and would not be isolated to the defense:

> Legal and political experts expect groups representing both the government and Microsoft to crank out more studies and analyses as the case quickly approaches the remedy phase. Their hope is to influence public opinion and public policy and possibly influence eventual remedies—what to do about Microsoft's alleged violation of antitrust laws—levied by a U.S. federal judge.[12]

The Koch-funded Cato Institute threw their hat in the ring by rereleasing a study by a fellow in the program, Robert Levy, which opposed the worst possible outcome for private business, the breakup of Microsoft. The results were in line with conservative ideology. Around that same time, and likely not by coincidence, the Progress and Freedom Foundation, itself a Washington, DC, think tank, issued its own proposal for how to go about breaking up the software conglomerate.

That was a time for counteracting statements, lobbying, and public opinion jockeying. The Association for Competitive Technology left the public opinion realm for a bit and got itself heard in the courtroom with a "friend of the court" brief not so shockingly in support of Microsoft. That early filing was later used to garner media attention around the legal experts who were in support of the defendant.

The advocacy groups would stay by Microsoft's side through thick and thin, as chronicled in CNET: "When in November U.S. District Judge

Thomas Penfield Jackson issued his stinging 'findings of fact' against Microsoft, [Citizens Against Government Waste] 'proclaimed today's 'finding of fact' ruling as a vindication of the Microsoft Corp. The ruling confirmed what Americans already know—that the software manufacturer is a tough competitor in a dynamic industry."[13]

The advocacy groups were everywhere, including the Computing Technology Industry Association, "which was founded in 1982 and represents more than 8,000 computer hardware and software manufacturers, distributors, retailers and system integrators, [and which] has also defended Microsoft. The group is generally viewed as an aggressive public policy mogul influencing technology legislation and regulation on Capitol Hill and in state houses across the United States."[14]

Nonetheless, the appellate court did not overrule the fact findings but did find that it was able to examine this type of highly technical industry within the framework of traditional antitrust analysis. Additionally, they remanded the case for consideration of a more fitting remedy with lesser liability.

As the case made its way through the courts, the *Los Angeles Times* revealed the most noteworthy dirty tactic by the Microsoft Corporation. Hundreds of similar letters were sent to newspapers articulating discontent with the government's efforts to rein in the tech giant. Those letters had been prepared by Americans for Technology Leadership and, in the most egregious cases, had been mailed from nonexistent addresses and dead people.

That piece would also go on to reveal that the founding members of Americans for Technology Leadership extended beyond Microsoft to several other advocacy groups, a handful of which were somehow also affiliated with the company, including Association for Competitive Technology; Citizens Against Government Waste; Cityscape Filmworks; Clarity Consulting; CompTIA; CompUSA; 60Plus Association; Small Business Survival Committee; and Staples, Inc.

Additionally, a specific campaign was aimed at the attorneys general of the twenty states who joined the DOJ in the suit through letters written to their offices on behalf of Microsoft. However, the nature of that effort was suspect, and not the innocent letter-writing campaign it was made to appear as.

This abject revelation was uncovered in detail in that August 2001 *Los Angeles Times* story by Joseph Menn and Edmund Sanders. The loose string was found in the beehive state, where Utah Attorney General Mark Shurtleff received roughly four hundred letters asking him to go easy on the corporation. It was suspicious at best and nefarious at worst that at least two of the letter writers were dead people.

The idea was to give the impression of a substantial grassroots movement in support of the conglomerate and potential monopoly. Once the true source was revealed, the efforts backfired, and plaintiffs were enraged. The effort had been put together by Americans for Technology Leadership and funded partly by Microsoft. The *Times* story went on to describe how the puppet masters behind the astroturf campaign were careful with how they put on the charade, saying that it, "goes to great lengths so that the letters appear to be spontaneous expressions from ordinary citizens. Letters sent in the last month are printed on personalized stationery using different wording, color and typefaces—details that distinguish those efforts from common lobbying tactics that go on in politics every day. Experts said there's little precedent for such an effort supported by a company defending itself against government accusations of illegal behavior."[15] The story quoted a University of California at Berkeley business professor as saying he had never seen anything of the like in his time.

The Justice Department regulators were first tipped off by realizations that similar, if not congruent, sentences were present in multiple letters and a not insignificant portion were marked with invalid return addresses. The Utah attorney general's office gave comment to the *Times*: "'It's an obvious corporate attempt to manipulate citizen input,' said Rick Cantrell, community relations director for the Utah attorney general. 'You can just tell these were engineered. When there's a real groundswell, people walk in, they fax, they call. We get handwritten letters.'"[16]

Through press releases, press conferences, and other tactics, the public and private sector foes looked to get the consensus on their side and hoped that popular opinion would find its way to influence the courtroom.

Microsoft attempted to defend themselves in the newspaper with a counterargument where Microsoft spokesman Vivek Varma was quoted as saying, "There's been a political campaign waged against Microsoft for a number of years by well-funded special interest companies like AOL, Oracle, Sun Microsystems and their trade associations." He added, "It's not surprising that companies and organizations that support Microsoft are mobilizing to counter that lobby."[17]

Those claims were obviously problematic as they did not acknowledge the extent to which the "companies and organizations that support Microsoft" could be simplified as "Microsoft." However, the allegation levied against competitors was not unfounded. Oracle had hired private investigators to go to Redmond and look into Microsoft, for instance, but those other software companies insisted they were not involving themselves in any way with the case in question.

When *Times* reporters Menn and Sanders went to Microsoft, they referred questions to Americans for Technology Leadership (ATL).

The process of how this campaign was crafted and the mechanics of the astroturfing were laid out in the *LA Times* exposé: "People working for ATL call residents and at first say they are conducting a poll about the Microsoft case. People who express support for Microsoft are sent letters to sign, along with handstamped, pre-addressed envelopes to their state attorney general, to President Bush and to their members of Congress."[18]

The executive director of Americans for Technology Leadership, Jim Prendergast, downplayed their involvement at first but was unable to ultimately deny that they wrote the letter for the constituents. Estimates from experts quoted in the *LA Times* put the price tag on the campaign as upwards of six-figures. Ultimately the goal was to sway members of Congress and empower or find protestors to force a friendly settlement ahead of more court time. It was a small part of their increased political and lobbying involvement, since having become the fifth-largest soft donor to both political parties in 1999 and 2000, as well as hiring numerous lobbyists and lobbying firms including Dewey Square Group and DCI/New Media.

Another Microsoft-supported group, Citizens Against Government Waste sent letters that spring to state offices where everything was identical aside from signatures.

Minnesota Attorney General Mike Hatch was quoted in the *LA Times* saying he got a few hundred letters and adding, "This is not a company that appears to be bothered by ethical boundaries."[19] State officials were insistent it would not impact their stance, likely only hardened by the revelation of the astroturf effort, and some even responded to the citizens. There were even instances of senders corresponding again and apologizing and explaining that they were duped.

Though some tactics were more advanced, there were ways to spot the falsification. Among them was letters to Iowa Attorney General Tom Miller that were not exact but bore major similarities. Four letters featured the exact sentence, "Strong competition and innovation have been the twin hallmarks of the technology industry" while another three had the exact phrasing, "If the future is going to be as successful as the recent past, the technology sector must remain free from excess regulation."[20]

Newsfactor, a technology focused blog, wrote about some of the specifics of the campaign and how Microsoft pulled it off. In a story that appeared on the site in August 2001 and just days after the *LA Times* had shined a light on the astroturfing, Nancy Clark, a spokesperson for Precision Communications, which works in political communications, suggested that Microsoft likely paid out to each organization behind the letter-writing campaigns on a "per-letter basis," adding that "Clark speculated that Microsoft may be shelling out as much as US$100,000 or more to have ATL, for example, generate 100 letters in each of the 18 states with lawsuits still pending against the company."[21]

The biggest splash from Newsfactor coverage came when they interviewed Carl Howe, principal analyst for Forrester Research. The analyst said that this tactic was used by the company previously, though it didn't particularly show with the sloppy execution and ultimate revelation. Howe was referring to events just after the trial began in which leaked documents revealed that the company had hired Edelman Public Relations, of "Wal-Marting Across America" infamy, to wage yet a different astroturf campaign.

"While the results of that effort were never as clearly documented as in this case, this is a tactic that Microsoft clearly understands," Howe told Newsfactor. "I don't think this is a wild idea. Some political campaigns have used the technique as well—hence the name for the category."[22]

Techrights, an advocacy group that "deals with a variety of issues that affect our everyday computing . . . by addressing particular subjects that need to be better understood and thus resolved," had their own take on the events.[23]

They pointed out the connections between advocacy groups and Microsoft, extending the umbrella to include Citizens Against Government Waste, DCI Group, and also a global alternative asset management company called The Carlyle Group. Microsoft was suspected to be behind those and more, including Association for Competitive Technology, which was exposed by Source Watch, which is published by the Center for Media and Democracy as a collaborative, online encyclopedia of organizations in the space.

A story in *The New York Times* alleged that the various trade groups were affiliated "to generate support for the company through Web sites and a sophisticated and largely hidden grassroots lobbying campaign."[24]

Techrights also looked to shed light on the undesirable tactics often used in this and many types of astroturfing efforts, which included: "changing names, shuffling umbrellas, and shifting their AstroTurfing budgets. . . . Once they get exposed for their interests, they can trivially morph by changing names and then seem more credible again. That's why it's important to keep track of immutable names of actual individuals."[25]

The connections between Americans for Technology Leadership and the Association for Competitive Technology (ACT) were not well masked, as the former's website, techleadership.org, is registered to the latter. One of the two people the site is registered to, Thomas J. Synhorst, through an LLC, TSE Enterprises, is a founding member of the aforementioned DCI Group, a strategic consulting and lobbying firm based in Washington, DC. Among the firm's prominent clients is Microsoft.

This complex web of connections is further detailed by Joshua Marshall in the July 17, 2000, issue of the nonprofit magazine *American Prospect*. Marshall wrote of the lobbying: "[W]hile Microsoft did confirm that Synhorst's DCI had been retained as a consultant, it insisted that another DCI employee, Tim Hyde, and not Synhorst, was handling the company's account. In any event, the web of connections among DCI, ATL, and Microsoft is striking. While working for Microsoft, DCI has also provided consulting services to ATL. And Josh Mathis, the man [ACT president Jonathan] Zuck installed as ATL's executive director, is also an employee of DCI, who still works out of the same Washington, DC, office as Synhorst and Hyde."[26]

In 2004, columnist Robert X. Cringley used his weekly PBS column "The Pulpit" to discuss how the tech giant had remained intact despite the government lawsuits, public relations failures, and backlash to a poorly constructed astroturfing campaign. The occasion was the settlement between Microsoft and Sun Microsystems, one of the chief Microsoft competitors that had been further weakened in their standing versus Goliath by the government and legal system's inability to harness the competition-crushing conglomerate.

He painted a harsh picture of a company with no weaknesses that was more powerful than the system set up to control it: "any legal system—is unequipped to change Microsoft's monopolistic behavior" the piece opined, "a few thousand readers out there expect me to blithely produce an answer to the problem of what to do to bring Microsoft into the civilized world. Well, I say it can't be done."[27]

The intervening time had done nothing to make those who viewed Microsoft as all-powerful any less distressed by their victories in the courtroom, "Where the governmental resolve would come to dissolve one of the greatest successes in world business is beyond me."[28]

The settlement with their competitor was more than a win for Microsoft, but nonetheless in an effort to continue to control competing technologies they put out a joint announcement saying: Microsoft and Sun will work together to improve collaboration between the Java and .Net technologies, while Microsoft will be allowed to continue to provide product support for the Microsoft Java Virtual Machine in its products. Microsoft was set to end support later this year, raising compatibility and security questions for users.[29]

At the time, the conventional wisdom was that Microsoft had reached checkmate. A dystopian picture was laid out by Cringley: "So what happens now that Microsoft is essentially unfettered thanks to a few payoffs and a $10 million per month legal bill. What I see coming is karmic retribution that begins with a phase I think of as 'the fleecing of the customers,' in which we will be forced to buy more and more stuff we don't really want or need."[30]

The story goes on to paint a picture of a longtime predatory company that was threatened, but ultimately emerged victorious and even, perhaps, strengthened. It even used a phrase in its infancy, "Silicon Valley":

> In Silicon Valley, hardware people look forward to the day someone like Cisco buys their company or technology and makes them rich. Software people fear the day that Microsoft notices their niche because they will get sucked dry. Some have even said that venture capital people are tending to avoid software companies . . . because Microsoft will pull a Netscape on you.[31]

To this day, the ultimate judgment has had an impact on the company. In its 2008 annual report, Microsoft said:

> Lawsuits brought by the U.S. Department of Justice, 18 states, and the District of Columbia in two separate actions were resolved through a Consent Decree that took effect in 2001 and a Final Judgment entered in 2002. These proceedings imposed various constraints on our Windows operating system businesses. These constraints include limits on certain contracting practices, mandated disclosure of certain software program interfaces and protocols, and rights for computer manufacturers to limit the visibility of certain Windows features in new PCs. We believe we are in full compliance with these rules. However, if we fail to comply with them, additional restrictions could be imposed on us that would adversely affect our business.[32]

CHAPTER 6
THE PHILIP MORRIS ALLIANCE

The National Smoker's Alliance formed in 1993 as an advocacy group in protest of anti-smoking legislation in the United States. Funded by the tobacco industry, it operated across the country from the year after its founding, 1994, to the end of the millennium, 1999. Siding with the allowance of adult tobacco use, they lobbied for deregulation and decreases in taxes on tobacco products.

The Alliance was ultimately revealed to be a front group for the Philip Morris Tobacco Company. Today, Phillip Morris USA is the producer of Marlboro, Virginia Slims, Benson & Hedges, Merit, Parliament, Alpine, Basic, Cambridge, Bucks, Dave's, Chesterfield, Collector's Choice, Commander, Lark, L&M, Players, Greensmoke, and MarkTen.

The purpose and inception of the National Smokers Alliance was an attempt to create a "grassroots opposition to smoke-free laws without its corporate involvement being detected."[1]

An article first published in *PR Watch*, authored by John C. Stauber and titled "Smokers' Hacks: the Tobacco Lobby's PR Front Groups," took a deep dive into the efforts of the National Smokers Alliance to achieve their goals.

The piece begins: "Recent news coverage might lead you to believe that tobacco is on its last legs, as its opponents lobby for aggressive public education and strict new regulations to prevent youthful addiction and to protect the public's right to a smoke-free environment. If you believe this, you're dead wrong, according to the chief PR lobbyist for the tobacco industry. Although tobacco's addicts are dying by the millions each year, sales are growing world-wide, says Thomas Lauria of the Tobacco Institute."

Lauria downplayed bad press about tobacco at a public relations seminar around the same time, saying critiques of tobacco were the latest "political correctness craze" and continuing on, he "ridiculed the predictions of tobacco's demise, saying that the media has been preparing smoking's obituary for decades."[2] He echoed ideas of tobacco locked in a never-ending battle, but nonetheless on a nearly perpetual win streak dating back to the cash crop of the South in the colonies.

There was validity to those claims, as industry profits were still on the climb as the industry shifted efforts to markets without regulation across the third world. Those were gains that were not entirely needed, as in the United States all attempts at regulation, or taxation, were being kept at arm's length by lobbyists on tobacco's dime.

With hopes to continue a winning streak for the ages, one of the most important tools at the tobacco companies' disposal was their lobbying monster: The National Smokers Alliance.

This was far from the first or only time the tobacco industry created a lobbying group. The earliest instance goes back to the 1950s with the Tobacco Institute Research Committee, formed by Hill & Knowlton. This original effort was but a preview of the well-funded, ambitious astroturf efforts of the National Smokers Alliance campaign.

Public relations company Burson-Marsteller drove the ship at the Alliance with funding from the Philip Morris Company. It was a trying time with the industry in the crosshairs of politicians and the Food and Drug Administration. Increased efforts at regulation were met with a countrywide mobilization that claimed to be, "bringing thousands of smokers into its ranks each week," as written in *PR Watch*.[3]

The public relations firm put their efforts toward a full court press. Full-page ads in newspapers nationwide, direct telemarketing, paid canvassing, 1-800 phone numbers, newsletters, and letters to federal agencies. These efforts were targeted at the fifty million Americans who smoke. The stated goal was "to rile-up and mobilize a committed cadre of hundreds of thousands, better yet millions, to be foot soldiers in a grassroots army directed by Philip Morris's political operatives at Burson-Marsteller," *PR Watch* wrote.[4] *PR Watch* put it bluntly, "The 'National Smokers Alliance' (NSA) is a sophisticated, hi-tech campaign that organizes tobacco's victims to protect tobacco's profits."[5]

The NSA focused on California, described as "the front line of the tobacco wars and the state where the industry has suffered its worst setbacks."[6] The Golden State was the target of a twenty million dollar effort to defeat an anti-smoking initiative in 1988, which was followed by hundreds of smoking bans across California. The regulations had the intended effect with a 30 percent decrease in smoking. At the time of publication in *PR Watch*, that represented the most success of any state in fighting big tobacco.

However, at the time Philip Morris and their alliance hadn't given up on the war. Brought into the efforts was a PR firm based in California, The Dolphin Group. With a reported half-million dollar offer from Philip Morris, an offshoot crafted in the image of the National Smokers Alliance was created: Californians for Statewide Smoking Restrictions. In an attempt to mislead petition signers, the group used their astroturf-incarnate moniker to garner a few hundred thousand signatures for a pro-smoking referendum in the election following the *PR Watch* story. It aimed to destroy in one fell swoop more than a hundred local anti-smoking ordinances across California.

"Philip Morris knows that to win a pro-smoking initiative it has to produce troops, people who can willingly argue on its behalf. The NSA is a sophisticated, camouflaged campaign that organizes tobacco's victims to protect tobacco's profits," Stauber wrote of the astroturfing.

Prior to this obvious astroturfing attempt, the tobacco industry was at least a bit more adept at keeping separate from pro-smoking lobbying. Brennan Dawson, of the aforementioned Tobacco Institute, echoed those denials in the *Congressional Quarterly* in 1990: "If we were to fund smokers' rights groups and bring them to Washington, wouldn't they then be viewed as an arm of the tobacco industry?"

Though that was the intention, perhaps the onslaught of opposition and desperation that resulted led to less professionalism. In a *National Journal* piece from 1994, Peter Stone wrote that the alliance "is increasingly looking like a subsidiary of Burson-Marsteller," and charged the PR firm with having "used its grassroots lobbying unit, the Advocacy Communications Team, to start building membership in the group last year."[7]

"Perhaps the tobacco industry is less concerned these days about fooling the news media, but it still appears important that the public not view the members of the NSA as pawns of Philip Morris or Burson Marsteller. Therefore, the names of the NSA's corporate funders and organizers are kept off of the group's materials," illustrated *PR Watch*.

With recruiting efforts ranging from high-tech direct marketing to simplistic local organizing to a newsletter titled *The NSA Voice*, they used all means at their disposal to grow their ranks; it was far from some simplistic grassroots group. The June 1994 issue of the newsletter detailed the NSA paying young people, namely college students, to sign up NSA members in American cities.

As an example of the success of these efforts, Eric Schippers, who was in charge of the membership drive, told *PR Watch* "during only the first two months of activity, the Chicago campaign put 180 recruiters on the street and enlisted more than 40,000 members."[8] That came with claims that NSA had 300,000 smokers on the rolls.

It was a very calculated step-by-step recruiting effort as laid out by *PR Watch*: "Many NSA members are first recruited via full-page ads with 800 numbers that exhort puffers to stand up for their rights. Everyone who calls receives the NSA newsletter free for three months, along with 10 membership recruitment cards and stickers to place in stores and restaurants that say, 'I am a smoker and have spent $_____ in your establishment.'"[9]

From there it is a bit like a pyramid scheme, with NSA members encouraged to sign up others to get a free shirt and a free 800 number with instructions on how to get further involved. An example of this in *PR Watch* was when the NSA targeted the Occupational Safety and Health Administration with a mailer sent out urging letters be written "to defeat new regulations that would 'BAN SMOKING IN ANY SITE WHERE WORK IS CONDUCTED.'"[10] They went as far as to call anti-smokers anti-American. A newsletter read: "If 'Anti' America is pushing a discriminatory smoking ban in your workplace, speak up . . . check the laws in your state with regard to the protection of individual rights."[11]

This was a game of survival for a company and industry backed into a corner. As *PR Watch* put it:

> Burson-Marsteller is more than happy to take the money that Philip Morris poured into its pro-smoking campaign, and Philip Morris has plenty of millions to spend. But this campaign is not really about swaying public opinion, a battle which the tobacco industry has already lost. Even half of the smokers say they favor stricter government regulation of their deadly habit.
>
> The tobacco industry's goal is not to win good PR, but to avoid losing political and legal battles. This survivalist strategy has served the cigarette industry well for forty years. The NSA provides Philip Morris with the shock troops they need to fight back at all levels . . . more and more PR firms will likely imitate B-M's technique of organizing front groups on behalf of their corporate clients.[12]

Newspapers covered the efforts of NSA to fight campaigns up and down the Pacific coast and across the nation. In 1996, the group launched a campaign in California to stop a state law aiming to ban smoking in bars.

The organization mailed posters, petitions, and coasters with their message to drinking establishments up and down California. Their aim was to bring awareness to bar owners, likely to oppose the law, as well as to amass signatures of support from the patrons at bars and taverns statewide to kill the bill by bringing the message from concerned citizens to the legislature.

Though the proposed ban became associated most strongly with taverns, a hot spot for indoor smoking at the time, it also prohibited smoking in most indoor workplaces and restaurants, though it did carve out a provision for freestanding drinking and eating establishments. The campaign was supported by many business owners due to the proposition that it could potentially cost them money and business.

The *Los Angeles Times*, in a 1996 story by Don Lee, characterized the opposition: "The National Smokers Alliance, formed in 1993 largely as a result of ever-stringent antismoking laws, says it has 3 million members, including 400,000 in California. Its corporate sponsors, which number fewer than 50, include tobacco firms such as Philip Morris Cos. Inc. and Brown & Williamson Tobacco Corp. as well as Fluor Daniel Inc. of Irvine."[13]

Among the most prominent members within the NSA ranks was Morton Downey Jr., of talk show fame. Not lacking for enthusiasm, Downey quit the habit halfway through the group's short shelf life, in 1996, when he was diagnosed with lung cancer. Three years later the alliance met its end when Philip Morris withdrew their funding in the aftermath of the group making an ethics complaint against Arizona Senator and then presidential candidate John McCain.

Born Sean Morton Downey, he hosted the eponymous *Morton Downey Jr. Show*. The show began in late 1987 as a regional program in New York and New Jersey. By the following year, his show expanded to national syndication. It was most well-known for the loud screaming matches between Downey and guests, which were even interspersed with contributions from the audience. It also became known for Downey's chain smoking as he flicked ash into a large silver bowl and at times blew smoke in the direction of guests. The iconic screaming gave birth to a cult following of "loud-mouths," as his fans called themselves.

Fostering tension among his guests and evoking anger were stalwarts as he railed against "pablum puking liberals" and told guests to "zip it."

The seminal profile of Downey's career came in 1988 when Tom Shales wrote about the firebrand in the *Washington Post*. It was suggestively titled, "SHRIEK! CHIC! IT'S MORTON DOWNEY!" The lead was equally verbose: "Suppose a maniac got hold of a talk show. Or need we suppose? The biggest splash in television right now is being made by 'The Morton Downey Jr. Show,' a nightly syndicated hour that is more slugfest than discussion, presided over by a host known for insulting, abusing and berating his guests, and sometimes having them thrown out of the studio by security guards."[14]

Aside from his antics, the story also discussed the significant, especially in a short timeline, influence and cultlike following he had quickly attained. His crowds were described as a "chanting horde of goonish Mortpackers who fill the seats in his studio each night." And as for how those crowds react to their fearless leader, "Mort greets one and all with the exhortation 'Let's kick ass'; they cheer so wildly they have to stand to do it."[15]

Just how real Downey's schtick was, according to the piece, was up for debate. Asked about the seemingly perpetual reservoir of anger, he said, "Sometimes now I'm not. Sometimes now I'm just irritated. Have I toned myself down from the beginning? Yeah, I think so. Sometimes I hear people in the audience whispering, 'Watch out, Mort's gonna go.' Well if I hear that, I don't go, because if I become predictable, then the Downey show is history."[16]

A part of his fodder was political in nature, including removing David Clarke, chairman of the Washington, DC, City Council, from his program.

"As for Downey's own political persuasion, it's hard to pin down" the *Post* story read. "I'm perceived as far-right usually . . . I am indeed a radical, but I'm a radical centrist. I think it's an identification that should be used more often. I see value in some liberal ideas, I see value in some conservative ideas. I see that the liberal ideas for 40 years haven't really worked," described Downey to Shales.[17]

He defended himself and his fan club to Shales: "No I don't think I'm a bully and certainly my audience is not a mob, either. You'll see guys coming in suits and jackets; they take them off, hide them under the chair. They're coming from Wall Street, Madison Avenue. I know some have come from the big advertising agencies and don't want their people to know they've been to the show. But it's a great audience. It says, 'Hey, here's Downey, he's exactly like I am, he's as frustrated as I am, only this sunuvabitch is doing something about it! So I'll let him say it for me, because I get my jollies that way, and by God he's saying the same thing I'd like to say.'"[18]

Words like demagoguery come to mind, but the only surefire charges are that of some serious and hastily garnered dedication of legions of riveted onlookers and passersby. Downey's rebuttal wasn't the most reassuring, either: "it's not demagoguery, it's a dictatorship."[19]

His appeal to the masses made him a useful pawn for the National Smokers Alliance prior to his reinvention. He believed his fan appeal came because he saw himself as a "loudmouth who gets in trouble just like they do, who's had problems just like they had, someone that they can identify with a lot more than someone who's squeaky clean."[20]

"One's instinct may be to deplore Downey, but then when you take a look at some of those who deplore him most vehemently, he becomes kind of appealing,"[21] Shales wrote. With all that considered, past connections with controversial presidential candidates George Wallace and Lyndon LaRouche didn't give much nuance to his characterization as a villain.

By late 1988, the shock value had seemingly worn off and Downey's ratings began to fall and the show was canceled in late 1989. The last episode was taped on June 30 and no new episodes were shown after September 15. After the failure of his show, Downey filed for bankruptcy in New Jersey in February 1990.

He launched several attempted comebacks with none ever taking off. The last of those attempts, in 1997, saw a different Downey than viewers were used to. Following surgery for lung cancer in which one of his lungs was removed, he appeared with a less confrontational and friendlier attitude. He quit the entertainment business for the final time on August 30, 1997, and only resurfaced in headlines for his legal battle with Howard Stern. Despite his early support of smoking, lung cancer had its effect and Downey was so upset by Stern allegedly spreading rumors he was still smoking that he took legal action against the fellow provocateur.

Upon his passing at sixty-seven years old, the major news outlets covered his escapades. He was described as "the chain-smoking, combative talk show host" by the Associated Press.[22] Smoking was a huge part of his profile; that same obituary described how "Downey, who lost a lung to cancer in 1996, was known for deliberately blowing smoke into the faces of guests who annoyed him. After his cancer surgery, however, he spent his final years as an anti-smoking advocate."[23]

It also went on to discuss how the change from a smoker to anti-smoking came in concert with a softening around the edges of his personality. In 1992, when he attempted to relaunch his career with a new project, he told the Associated Press of the venture: "No meanness this time. Just as confrontational, just as tough, just as opinionated, but everyone else has the right to have their opinion and be heard."[24]

Downey tried to absolve himself of all the blame for that troublesome behavior, saying in an interview in 1995 that: "It got out of control because the producers . . . wanted me to top myself every night . . . If I did something outlandish on Monday night, on Tuesday night, we'd have to think of something even more outlandish."[25]

A *New York Times* obituary echoed similar sentiments, describing the notorious host as having a "loudmouthed manner and sneering, smoke-in-your-face approach to guests on his television show [that] gave him a wildly popular, albeit short, career as a national talk show host in the 1980's." They additionally reported the cause of death as "lung cancer and other respiratory ailments."[26] Even with some damning interpretations, the transformation he made later in life made the page. As the *Times* put it, "He lost one lung to cancer in 1996, after which he became a crusader against tobacco, appearing on television shows to spread his message."

The inextricable link between smoking and Downey was across the obit pages; in the *Washington Post*, they wrote of his calling card as "the growling and opinionated TV talk-show host who shocked viewers from behind a haze of cigarette smoke." It continued: "A chain smoker for years until losing a lung to cancer, Mr. Downey was known for deliberately blowing smoke into the faces of guests who annoyed him when he was host of one of the most popular talk shows on television." His transformation was also covered by other publications who chronicled his death, including the *Post* saying: "After his cancer surgery in 1996, he became an anti-smoking crusader. Saying he had been 'an idiot' for smoking, he taped public service announcements and told the syndicated TV show 'Extra' that he hoped he could 'undo some of the damage that I did during all the years that I did television' . . . Years later, Mr. Downey would acknowledge that he probably carried things too far."[27]

In March 2001, just a short time before his death, Downey discussed his regrets on an episode of *Larry King Live*. He told the host, "I had spawned a generation of kids to think it was cool to smoke a cigarette. Kids walked up to me until a matter of weeks ago, they'd have a cigarette in their hand

and they'd say, 'Hey, Mort,' or, 'Hey, Mouth, autograph my cigarette.' And I'd do it."[28]

Downey's private life struggles were on par with his professional career. He was married four times and had four children from three of the four marriages. His lung cancer diagnosis came during treatment for pneumonia.

In the early going, the loud mouth talk show host was on the side of smokes. That was changed by lung cancer. Put plainly in a *Los Angeles Times* lead by Myron Levin in the summer of 1996: "Morton Downey Jr. has gone from smokers' rights advocate to anti-smoking crusader. Lung cancer can do that to you."[29]

The abrasive talk show host and overnight Hollywood star had been a heavy smoker most of his life prior to diagnosis, but cancer was enough to flip his staunch smoking stance. Days before surgery to remove a lung and save his life he met with the American Lung Association at a Los Angeles news conference and unveiled an anti-smoking advertisement for the Association featuring himself and his young daughter. He was contrite and described himself as a "sucker" and "fool," the types of terms previously reserved for guests on his show with whom he disagreed.

"In the 30-second commercial, Downey, seated on a playground swing next to his young daughter, introduces himself as the "television tough guy" who "knew cigarettes could never hurt me."

"Now I've got lung cancer, and I could die," he says. "What really bothers me is I won't be around to see my 2 1/2-year-old to say, 'No to smoking.'"

He had been a board member of the NSA just months prior, but the life-changing condition had changed that. He took the opportunity at the public event to switch teams, taking the side of industry scientists, lobbyists, cigarette models, and other prominent figures who had at one time fought for smoking but came to see the same light.

Downey came for the National Smokers Alliance with guns blazing. "Downey acknowledged that until recently, he thought the real problem was groups such as the lung association, making it harder for smokers to indulge their habit,"[30] the *LA Times* piece said. It went on to show his dynamic nature by adding a quote from the man himself about the organization he now sat side by side with: "I still think they're zealots . . . I think I'm one of the zealots with them."[31]

He decried the Alliance, at the time the most prominent pro-smoking organization, by describing it as a "total front" for the tobacco industry and a "nothing organization" comprised of "minimal grass-roots support" that was "designed to frighten Congress into thinking" millions of active members shared their cause. Downey said the actual number of active members paled in comparison.

The Alliance didn't take that sitting down. They responded to the host: "Told of Downey's remarks, alliance Vice President Gary Auxier said: 'If we are a front group at all, we are a front group for 3 million adult American smokers.'"[32]

The back and forth continued, but on Downey's part it was full of regret. "I used a cigarette as a combat weapon, and I never gave much thought to the [chance] that this cigarette would most likely kill me,"[33] Downey said.

"Was I part of the problem? You bet I was," Downey was quoted in the *Times* piece as saying, and he added that he wanted to "do something for those kids along the way who I made think smoking was cool."[34]

According to Downey, he left the Alliance board prior to the diagnosis. In a letter of resignation, he said he described himself as "a person who is tragically addicted to smoking cigarettes." Impacting his decision was the denials of nicotine addiction from the industry. It gave him the realization that he was "no longer confident that the information imparted by the tobacco manufacturers and the NSA reflects the truth."[35]

The anti-smoking movement that prompted the NSA's creation could be traced back to a 387-page document released by Surgeon General Luther L. Terry in 1964. The first official document linking cigarettes to disease, it said, "Cigarette smoking is a health hazard of sufficient importance in the United States to warrant appropriate remedial action."[36]

In the typical pace of democracy, government, and legislation, it took more than a quarter century for the federal government and regulatory bodies to attempt to use these revelations to spur action. The FDA rules were a seminal moment in that national change of heart. As described in a 1996 piece by Glenn Frankel, which appeared in the *Washington Post*:

[A]nti-smoking activists and tobacco industry officials alike agree that the Food and Drug Administration rules announced yesterday amount to a watershed moment in which the federal government, after decades of false starts, conflict and delay, has finally chosen to move decisively to restrict a product that health experts consider America's primary cause of preventable disease and death.[37]

Matthew Myers, general counsel for the Center for Tobacco-Free Children, told the *Post*, "Thirty-two years after the surgeon general's first report, the government has finally replaced rhetoric with substance."[38]

As would be the case whenever regulations began to appear, the NSA was on the case. NSA President Thomas Humber was quoted in the same story as saying, "It is the epitome of the slippery slope . . . Someone smart figured out that this is a first acceptable step. This is not where [FDA Commissioner] David Kessler wishes to stop."[39]

The counter campaign from the industry against these rules came on all fronts. From a lawsuit in North Carolina Federal Court to efforts to impact the voting polls to Washington, DC, where they made huge financial investments, they were a force to be reckoned with. However, time had eroded their hold. Frankel wrote, "But even in Congress, their dominance is now in dispute. Industry lobbyists privately concede they are uncertain whether they can muster the votes to overturn or preempt the FDA, and anti-tobacco activists are expressing new confidence."[40]

The tides were turning and momentum was at the backs of anti-smoking advocates by the fall of 1997. On September 21, Tom Kuntz wrote about the still fervent pro-smoking "Resistance" in the *New York Times*. It came as no surprise that "defenders of smoking aren't taking things lying down." And the example he used of this movement, you guessed it, was the National Smokers Alliance. He carefully ascribed them as "claiming 3 million members" while not shying away from saying that the group "gets much of its financial support from tobacco companies."[41]

Kuntz used the words from the NSA's own newsletters, namely *The NSA Voice* and *The Resistance*, to ascribe an ideology to those fighting for the right to smoke. In the inaugural issue of the latter publication, the term resistance, in that case resisting laws against smoking, was compared to the French resistance groups during World War II when the country was occupied by the Nazi Party: "It has happened in many other countries, in many other circumstances and under many other names, but the Resistance has always been the last line of defense against those who would impose their will on a minority."[42]

They cited instances where smoking bans were disobeyed as brave stands against tyranny by referencing a smoking law in Toronto that local businesses refused to enforce, instead eating sizable fines upwards of a few thousand dollars.

They knew their enemy well and in *The NSA Voice* they went after scientific findings opposite to their stance and also told horror stories of smoking bans reducing great municipalities to barren wastelands. For that they cited Mesa, Arizona, where a smoking ban was in place in a majority of public places. They made claims of dying businesses left and right as a result and even found a connection to a lack of charity money to buy underprivileged children Christmas presents. All because of less smoking, who knew?

As is commonplace in cultural debates, they blamed pop-culture for many ills. In the May 1996 *NSA Voice* they countered arguments against smoking in movies by citing the vulgarity and brutality of *Pulp Fiction*, a film by notoriously controversial director Quentin Tarantino.

Above all, the most important message to their astroturfing was the political pull smokers held. They had a promotion titled "More Americans Smoke Than Voted for Clinton," featuring bumper stickers that served as a reminder to politicians that the country had fifty million smokers and the NSA gladly classified them all loosely as members (just don't check the fine print).

They even took the fight to smokers who weren't all in on their side of the fight. In an *NSA Voice* article by a member of the advisory board of the Smokers' Alliance, Bruce Herschensohn wrote: "Frequently in interviews with smokers on television and radio and in the press, the smoker doesn't talk about liberty and personal choice at all but, rather, the smoker gives ammunition to the other side. Just imagine what would have happened if the battles of other minorities were fought as this one is being fought." He went on to compare the oppression and causes of smokers to those of African Americans and Jewish people before finishing with: "Too many people who enjoy smoking are bringing about their own restrictions by their sheepishness and their inability to express the real issues that are at risk in the United States."[43]

That particular piece of propaganda concludes with comparing President George H. W. Bush's affinity for skydiving, the dangers of skiing, and the free will of an American to smoke cigarettes based on one Chinese man who smoked all his life and lived to 93.

The last example cited by Kuntz, after surely combing through lots of fodder for astroturfing, is an appeal to the romantic in all of us. He told the story of a couple who met on a smoke break before editorializing, "Like too many workplaces nationwide, smoking is prohibited inside at the State of Tennessee's Department of Mental Health, where John and Betty work. John, a quality director, and Betty, a secretary, work in separate divisions."[44] Well if that doesn't just break your heart. Never mind the fact that since they work in different divisions, they most likely never would have met if their company didn't prohibit smoking and force them outside.

Myron Levin was still writing about the largest smoking advocacy group in the country in 1998 when he dove into their tax records to show just how much "grassroots" effort was present, only to confirm his hypothesis that the grass was more astroturf.

The *Times* cited "minimal support from the 3 million people it claims as members" and through the exploration of public records found "its only significant backer is Big Tobacco."[45]

On the contrary, as the group fought it claimed it was, "a nonprofit, grass-roots membership organization with more than 3 million members"[46] in group brochures, a claim parroted in reports by major news organizations. The members who would be necessary for an actual grassroots movement, however, were not as strongly aligned as the tobacco companies, which had a horse in the race. Despite coffers of $45.9 million, few of the members paid the $10 dues. In 1996 the group had receipts totaling $9 million but only $74,000 in dues, which paints a picture of a group of only 7,400 members.

As for bigger donors, "Internal documents reviewed by The Times show that of the first $7 million funneled to the alliance after its founding in August 1993, nearly all came from giant Philip Morris Cos."[47]

The group wisely deflected these lines of inquiry, only conceding to the original seed money from Philip Morris but insisting that in the intervening time members got involved and, along with corporate contributions, kept them afloat. The reality is very different, according to Levin: "Facing increasing hostility from nonsmokers, as well as mounting restrictions on where they can light up, the nation's 48 million smokers would appear to be a potent political force. But experts say a large majority of smokers want to quit, and rather than fighting back tend to regard bans as the medicine they need."[48]

"In many prominent battles, however, the smokers' alliance has put itself forward as the voice of abused smokers rather than as a mouthpiece for the industry," the *Times* said before describing the notable players:

> The group was launched by Philip Morris and Burson-Marsteller, the tobacco giant's longtime public relations firm. The two directors named in its incorporation papers were both lawyers with Hunton & Williams, a Richmond, Va., law firm that represents Philip Morris. The alliance's interim president, David K. McCloud, was a Burson-Marsteller executive.[49]

McCloud was succeeded by Thomas Humber, a fellow Burson executive who had worked for Philip Morris in Switzerland and earlier for Brown & Williamson Tobacco Corp.

Humber earned $450,731 as president and CEO of the alliance during the year ended September 30, 1996, according to the group's report to the IRS.[50]

With the limited financial information available, just how much the group was a stooge of big tobacco was unclear, but Levin did find some clues. In the last two reporting years in 1998, less than one percent of the group's funds came from dues and of the first $4 million the group received as of early 1994, 96 percent came from Philip Morris. Later that year the company would contribute an additional $3 million.

A microscopic example of the on-the-ground efforts by interest groups can be found in June 1998 in Sacramento, California. As the state assembly weighed a pair of smoking-related regulations, there was a backdrop of "heavy lobbying by tobacco representatives, and a significant showing by bar owners organized by the National Smokers' Alliance, a group largely funded by the tobacco industry,"[51] as Dan Morain wrote in the *Los Angeles Times*.

This was just the latest battle and the Alliance was in it for the long haul having been lobbying against the ban since January 1, 1998, when it went into effect. Their power was demonstrable as California Labor Federation President Tom Rankin argued that a proposed bill pushed forward in the state was too friendly to tobacco interests.

CHAPTER 7
NOT-SO-CLEAN COAL

The American Coalition for Clean Coal Electricity (ACCCE) was founded in 2008 as a nonprofit advocacy group representing the interests of coal, utility, and railroad companies. It started due to the Center for Energy and Economic Development (CEED) and Americans for Balanced Energy Choices (ABEC) combining. The former had been around since 1992 and focused on climate and energy policies that impacted coal-based electricity companies. The latter came about in 2000 with a focus on consumer-based advocacy efforts in the same sector.

Their mission is to influence public opinion and, in turn, legislation, to support the coal industry across the United States. However, their advocacy is an uphill battle as the chief tactic they get behind, clean coal technologies, remains questionable in applicability and possibility.

When combined in 2008, the two groups focused on legislation and advocacy with the "America's Power" initiative, which was launched by ABEC in 2007 before the merger and continued its relevance in the 2008 and 2012 election cycles. Exposure of dishonest practices, aka astroturfing, was discovered as a chief tactic that came about in the debate over the Waxman-Markey cap and trade legislation in the United States House of Representatives. That bill aimed to set up a cap and trade system similar to the system in the European Union. This would put a limit on how much the country could emit greenhouse gases and allow industry players to buy and trade allowances for emissions.

ACCCE faced a congressional investigation when it was exposed that a lobbying firm hired them to send forged letters to lawmakers. The letters were made to appear as though they came from minority-focused nonprofit groups, but they actually came from the special interests and their lobbying efforts.

Affiliates of the coalition include Peabody Energy, Southern Company, American Electric Power, and CSX Transportation, along with thirty-four total member groups. They are headquartered in Washington, DC.

The aforementioned scandal surrounded the climate change legislation that aimed to cap greenhouse gas emissions along with allowing trading of emission allowances. ACCCE opposed the law, with their support instead behind questionable clean coal technologies. They opposed allowances and supported a ceiling on emission allowance prices.

Prior to Waxman-Markey, the United States Senate was taking up the Lieberman-Warner bill under consideration as the mechanism for cap and trade installation. This bill would similarly set up cap and trade with a goal of tightening restrictions over time. The coalition fought for coal's inclusion as the main energy source within that policy but did not come out expressly against the bill.

Ads appeared early on that prefaced the first climate change bill sponsored by Senator Joe Lieberman of Connecticut and Senator John Warner of Virginia.

"Big coal may launch a 'Harry and Louise'-style disinformation campaign to sink global warming solutions in Congress,"[1] said Daniel J. Weiss, senior fellow and director of climate strategy for the Center for American Progress to the *Washington Post*, channeling an ad campaign by the healthcare industry that took down healthcare proposals while Bill Clinton was in office.

A radio ad additionally spread big coal's message by asking: "How can we become less dependent on foreign resources? What fuels will keep power bills reasonable and be environmentally responsible?" In response, biased answers were given: "We have many questions for our candidates, and coal has to be part of the discussion." The ABEC's executive director Joe Lucas boasted, "We're getting the message out."[2]

As the debate waged on, a capital-based lobbying firm, Bonner & Associates, worked with ACCCE through the Hawthorn Group in an effort to foster grassroots support for their cause. In that push, they sent a number of letters to lawmakers on behalf of the group from various advocacy groups that were specifically in the space of nonprofit and minority advocacy, including such prevalent organizations as the National Association for the Advancement of Colored People and the American Association of University Women.

Yet ultimately, the bill's final version did not appeal to pro-coal desires or rally the support of their lobby, despite all the attempts.

The bill's success and, in turn, the coalition's failure to enact their agenda did not slow down advocates opposed to ACCCE in all its iterations. Some prominent advocates on the other side include the Sierra Club and Greenpeace.

"We welcome a vigorous debate about our energy future and solving global warming. Unfortunately ABEC is spending millions of dollars on misinformation about our energy choices . . . instead of engaging in a real debate about the true costs of coal and clean energy alternatives," said Bruce Nilles, director of the Sierra Club's national coal campaign to the *Post*.[3]

"Both the coal industry's ACCCE and Bonner have denounced the sneaky tactics and firmly placed blame elsewhere," Sierra Club executive director Carl Pope was quoted as saying in the *New York Times*. "It is clear that the Department of Justice and Congress may be the only ones that can really figure out who is responsible for these dirty tricks."[4]

He added: "Big Oil, Big Coal and other special interests have already spent more than $100 million to kill a comprehensive clean energy jobs and climate plan. By faking these letters, Bonner and the special interests they represent admit that an army of lobbyists and hundreds of millions of dollars still can't overcome real grassroots power."[5]

The Sierra Club would go on to run counter ads mocking the arguments of the other side and the validity of their scientific claims.

Both groups were among the chorus of voices questioning the validity of claims that a version of coal that is "clean," environmentally speaking, is viable or scientifically possible. If possible, the groups felt the time and budget to find those technologies should be funded by the coal industry.

In 2009 with the Waxman-Markey cap and trade legislation, those for coal felt differently, expressing fervent, robust opposition. The group argued that the proposed regulations would reduce employment with increases in energy expenses. This argument came with the economy in the grips of a recession, started just years earlier and with no end in sight.

The group also took their efforts to the streets with consumer advocacy, responding to the debate over the environmental impact of coal and their pet project, clean coal. They employed direct advertising, brought together 225,000 volunteers who made up "America's Power Army," and, according to their site, those members attended town halls and other get-togethers featuring legislators to speak about energy policy.

The opposition efforts spared no expense, with proposals provided to congressional members for legislative adjustments. They also approved changes that were in the works and supported their side of the discussion. They also sent those letters to lawmakers.

Those letters turned out to be forged.

After these fraudulent activities came to light, a congressional investigation followed and ACCCE apologized to the groups they embroiled in the controversy and the members of Congress whom had been recipients of the astroturf documents. Additionally, they disavowed the methods and blamed the groups with whom they had gotten involved. The blame game was passed on to a temporary worker who was said to have acted alone, nothing suspicious there.

Representative Edward Markey, who helped create the bill that spurred the opposition, launched an investigation into the acts and disclosed even more fake letters that had gotten into the hands of lawmakers, all of which expressly opposed the environmentally conscious legislation. This time around, the coalition seemed a bit more remorseful, although first impressions and reactions go a long way. They pledged to take all necessary steps to ensure the validity of all the letters sent out by Bonner & Associates on behalf of ACCCE and made their cooperation with the investigation pronounced. At the conclusion of Markey's investigation in October 2009, Bonner & Associates Chairman Jack Bonner bore the brunt of the responsibility.

Scrutiny had come earlier, as it was not the first time the advocacy group had lobbied in a suspect manner. In the aftermath of the 2008 Presidential Election there were claims that both candidates, Barack Obama and John McCain, had their positions altered based on the coalition's presence at the Democratic and Republican National Conventions.

In January 2008, with the presidential and various other general elections looming at year's end, ACCCE and various allied advocacy groups put together a campaign of $35 million across primaries and caucuses in order to garner public support for the coal industry and oppose the legislation threatening the industry in the name of climate change.

According to a story from the *Washington Post* by Steven Mufson, ABEC, spent $1.3 million on ads in the integral early ballot states of Iowa, Nevada, and South Carolina, spreading their message across billboards, newspapers, television, and radio.[6]

An example of those advertisements can be found in a television spot showing a power cord plugged into a lump of coal. It referred to the fossil fuel as "an American resource that will help us with vital energy security" as well as "the fuel that powers our way of life," and it pointed out that half of the nation's electricity is produced at coal-fired plants.[7]

They brought their efforts on the road with some fifty people, many paid, taking to the campaign trail, including a Democratic debate in Nevada. ABEC Executive Director Joe Lucas told Mufson, on a stop between Nevada and South Carolina, that, "in Iowa, there is a saying that you don't get to be president unless you go through Iowa. We'd like to say that you don't get to be president unless you understand how complicated this issue is."[8]

The *Post* story went on to detail the precarious position for an antiquated industry that prompted the nefarious initiative:

> The group's message—that coal-fired power plants can be clean, and that more of them are needed to meet the growing demand for electricity—comes when opposition to new coal plants is mounting because they generate greenhouse gases. In Kansas, where a state agency rejected a permit for two proposed coal plants, opinion polls show that roughly two out of three people opposed the plants. That sentiment, plus soaring construction costs and uncertainty about federal climate change legislation, last year prompted U.S. companies to abandon or postpone plans to build dozens of new coal plants.[9]

The combined coal support groups also had allies in the National Mining Association with its $19.7 million budget. ABEC also boasted a big budget that quadrupled with help from the aforementioned backers.

The 2008 presidential campaign posed a problem for the coal industry and power plants that run on them in both Obama and McCain, a problem that the president finishing out his term, George W. Bush, had not presented. The senators were both in support of putting caps on greenhouse gases emitting from major polluting industries. With power plants running on coal both producing half the country's electricity and leading all industries in emissions of the main greenhouse gas, carbon dioxide, it was clear that big coal and the presidential candidates were not seeing eye to eye, according to reports at the time by the Government Accountability Office.[10]

As the election approached, the candidates started to open their minds to clean coal, according to a piece in the *Wall Street Journal*.[11]

At the time, Stephen Miller was serving as president of ACCCE and the lobbying group's tab had reached more than $40 million alone on outreach efforts. Their chief argument was an economic one: coal is the cheapest option.

The candidates' changes of heart and shifting of priorities was far from natural; on the contrary, it was costly. At the Democrat and Republican National Conventions, ACCCE spent close to $2 million on advertising, from conventional means to advocates on the streets. Those efforts were not isolated to the political meccas but appeared at town halls nationwide where coal support was cultivated on behalf of—and at the expense of—ACCCE.

The profound impact of those efforts was evident when looked at through the proper lens. During a rally on the campaign trail, Obama said that he would support clean ways to store coal, which are scientifically suspect. The efforts had gotten to the unlikeliest of susceptible parties: the man who would eventually serve as president and sign the Paris Agreement on working to prevent climate change. Obama even used his support of coal as an example of his individuality from his party in the final debate.

Just how they operated was evidenced in a saga between ACCCE President Miller and Obama's running mate, Senator Joe Biden, chronicled in the *WSJ* story by Power: "In September, Sen. Obama's running mate, Delaware Sen. Joe Biden, drew concern from coal country when he suggested that an Obama-Biden administration wouldn't support 'clean coal' technology. Mr. Miller says he called Sen. Biden's office, urging him to 'clarify' his comments in a way that 'expresses his support for a significant future role for coal in this country.' Mr. Miller also alerted local Democratic officeholders in coal-abundant states such as Pennsylvania, Colorado and Virginia, whose electoral votes are seen as pivotal to the outcome of the race."[12]

Three days later, the campaign issued a clarifying statement, according to the *Wall Street Journal*, saying that the candidates "support clean coal technology." That went even further with the announcement of a clean coal jobs task force just days later.[13]

Both sides of the ballot were susceptible to the push and pull of ACCCE and the powerful sector they worked for, and not in a transparent manner.

Both candidates had been critical of coal and the coal industry in the past, both in words and in positions. Despite that, they suddenly both supported technological advancements aimed at storing carbon emissions from coal plants. Relevant experts and agencies, as well as the United States Department of Energy, still doubted the necessary measures were cost efficient.

Miller was ready for a battle, quoted in the *Journal* as saying, "Whichever [candidate] is elected is going to recognize this nation is going to use coal for many decades to come. Where they may have been a year ago on this issue is not where they are now."[14]

"Yes, we do need to be more energy efficient," conceded Lucas in the *Post*, adding, "but even as we become more efficient, we're plugging more things into the wall."[15] Coal plants had become more efficient and environmentally clean as a result of regulations, but they still remained major emitters of climate-harming chemicals. However, friends of coal framed it as the former being worthier of focus than the latter. A newspaper ad neglected to mention carbon dioxide, the chief troublesome chemical inextricable from the process of burning coal and said that coal plants were "70 percent cleaner based on regulated emissions per unit of energy produced."[16]

The ads quite obviously focused on the pros, not the cons, of coal, and therefore neglected a huge part of the picture. Among the positives they chose to highlight was coal's cheap price tag in comparison to many alternative forms of energy. This was true, but it ignored that prices were on the rise and that many opponents were not concerned with the price in dollars anyway, but the price in pollution.

The main battlefront, however, remained the Waxman-Markey Bill, also known as House Resolution 2454 or the American Clean Energy and Security Act of 2009. It had become known (as many bills are) by its authors, Democrats Henry A. Waxman of California and Edward J. Markey of Massachusetts.

In response came the letter-writing campaign as detailed in the *New York Times,* targeting three members of Congress who received letters opposing the climate bill in the House, all of whom were Democrats: Tom Perriello of Virginia and Kathy Dahlkemper and Chris Carney of Pennsylvania. The latter pair would vote against the bill while Perriello would support it and face backlash from Republicans and constituents alike. ACCCE was identified as the culprit behind the letters.

Upon denying their involvement, and placing the blame on Bonner & Associates, ACCCE President and CEO Stephen Miller said in a statement, "We are outraged at the conduct of Bonner & Associates . . . Based upon the information we have, it is clear that an employee of Bonner's firm failed to demonstrate the integrity we demand of all our contractors and subcontractors."[17]

The *New York Times* reported that the original discovery of the forgery came from an internal review conducted by Bonner and then brought to the attention of Hawthorn Group. Those discoveries made their way to the ACCCE a month before being discovered by the media.

Miller, however, insisted that the group was unaware and once they were informed they aimed to remedy the situation by clarifying with the community groups and congressional offices implicated. However, the attempts to rectify the situation somehow went awry. "As we continued to inquire about that during July, that was the message we received from Hawthorn [the message blaming Bonner]," Miller said in the *Times*. "It was not until the press accounts Friday afternoon that we learned this matter had not been dealt with."[18] He added that Bonner had fired the employees responsible, according to ACCCE's information and that he had visited the offices of congressional members involved and would be attempting to meet in person or speak on the phone to clarify and would also do the same with community groups.

A congressional investigation followed, led by Representative Markey, who had also authored the bill that set off the fraud-based astroturfing. Markey questioned Bonner about the lobbying efforts and who paid for them and how much they cost.

"This fraud on Congress distorts the legislative process and deceives the American people," Markey wrote in a letter to Jack Bonner of Bonner & Associates. "It represents a serious breach that needs to be fully understood as to the extent and scope of these wrongful acts."

As *New York Times* reporter Alex Kaplun laid out, "The letters have only further escalated what has already been a highly charged political debate over the climate legislation. Besides Markey's investigation and similar calls from the Sierra Club, a number of other left-leaning advocacy groups and commentators had pounced on the issue, charging that the letters were part of a campaign by some industry groups that used inaccurate information to attempt to defeat the climate bill."[19]

"I continue to have faith that when a problem like this occurs and it's not your wrongdoing yourself, but you're willing to step up responsibility for making it right, people will recognize that here in Washington," Miller said in the *Times*. "I hope and believe that if you're willing to do that and come forward in this kind of situation, you will continue to be able to make credible arguments."[20]

A story in the *Wall Street Journal* by Jeffrey Ball talked about the coal industry that sat at the crux of this astroturfing and its resistance: "Coal, more than any other fuel, powers the planet . . . Coal's problem is that it is dirty. When burned, it spews out more carbon dioxide than any other fossil fuel."[21]

The same story discussed the principal proposal of clean coal that, "refers to the idea of harnessing the black rock's energy while safely disposing of the resulting CO_2 rather than sending it skyward."[22] He pointed out the big problem for that proposal: "Right now, clean coal seems both possible and improbable. The basic elements of clean coal are already in use in small corners of industry. But whether it is broadly and quickly adopted around the world will depend less on science than on economics. Cleaning coal is very expensive."[23]

As an example of the problem at hand, Ball used the Pleasant Prairie power plant in Wisconsin as a microcosm of the debate and example of the issue. The plant was one of the most advanced in terms of clean emissions and energy efficiency after three decades in business. As new environmental rules came along, the plant adapted, burning roughly thirteen thousand tons of coal daily to account for 13 percent of Wisconsin's electricity intake.

At the time of the story, new rooms were being added with pollution-reducing machinery and, according to Ball's account, "half as much space at the plant is devoted to preventing pollution as to producing power. That has slashed the plant's output of chemicals that cause respiratory disease and acid rain."[24] Those efforts were hyperbolized by one side, but were seemingly not enough for the counterpoints on the other side. "But it has done nothing to trim the plant's emissions of CO_2. This coal-fired power plant is cleaner than it once was, but it still isn't 'clean.' This plant pours out some 8.6 million tons of CO_2 annually—about as much as 1.7 million U.S. cars."[25]

At the time of that story, capturing CO_2 was not commonplace and when it was done it was for government incentives with steam power or for use in soft drinks or freezing food.

The plant in question was experimenting with CO_2 capture in the first quarter of 2009. A three-story tall machine was only grabbing one percent of greenhouse gases and ultimately was not successful in its energy-in-energy-out distribution. That plant was still only in the beginning stages, as capturing the carbon was only step one since it also had to be disposed of safely. They were not alone, as only one percent of the coal in the country at the time, six billion tons, was being taken care of properly by being injected into wells.

In the same story, clean coal specialist at Massachusetts Institute of Technology Howard Herzog's plan to fix the problem was introduced, but it was also quoted at $1 billion a year solely for research.

Around the same time as experts were making a push, in the months around the 2008 election, anti-coal sentiment was gaining steam. Herzog was a fan of compromise in the form of clean coal and technology. But the prices were tough to see going into action. Just earlier that year the federal government had conducted research into a carbon-free coal plant and the price ultimately led to both the idea and the plant being shut down.

It all came back to Pleasant Prairie where regulation met expense and no clear solution was present, but the coal kept burning.

In between the election efforts and the letter-writing campaign in response to the Waxman-Markey bill, Ari Berman wrote an exposé on ACCCE in the *Nation*. The lead summed up the eternal struggle between the advocates and the public consensus on coal: "Yet the American coal industry, which pumps 2 billion tons of CO_2 into the atmosphere each year and contributes more than one-third of the nation's overall greenhouse gas emissions, is nothing if not resilient. Despite rising public concern about global warming and a growing awareness that coal is an irrevocably dirty business, the industry is spending millions of dollars on a slick messaging campaign."[26]

While coal advocates discussed the potential improvements that could be found in clean coal advancements, those opposed said that terminology was vague and out of touch with reality. The studies backed opponents up, with none of the 616 coal plants across the country being "carbon-free" or anywhere near it. According to the Center for American Progress, the biggest coal companies in the United States were spending a minuscule portion of the billions of dollars at their disposal toward developing technologies to reduce emissions from coal plants. The Center gave a damning assessment, saying, "The ads and other public clean coal activities are merely designed to delay global warming solutions without suffering a public relations black eye."[27]

With Obama winning the 2008 election, a stimulus package for an ailing economy came along and was clearly skewed toward green energy advancements and against the type of actions that would exacerbate climate change. Coal, and the clean coal argument, were at the center of the debate. In the *Nation*, the questions central to the future of United States energy policy were spelled out:

> How serious is the industry about developing clean coal, and can it happen? Does the latest message indicate a more environmentally friendly policy, or just a crafty makeover? Can the same people who told us that global warming didn't exist—or that it was a good thing—suddenly be trusted to help solve the climate crisis?[28]

ACCCE and its $40 million purse were the centerpiece of coal's rebranding attempt. They had all the trimmings of a top-notch K street lobbying group with a downtown Washington office and a top lobbyist in Paul Bailey, who had experience with similar efforts for the oil and electric industries, along with plans to hire more executives. This was a step up for an already powerful group. Other offices were in Virginia on John Carlyle Street at the former home of their forebears: radical climate change–denying organizations, such as the Western Fuels Association and the Greening Earth Society, out of which the cleaner cut, but just as steadfast, ACCCE grew.

This fight against global warming dated back quite some time. In 1992, President George H. W. Bush attended an international climate change conference in Brazil that was the first step toward the Kyoto Protocol, a 1992 international treaty extending the 1992 United Nations Framework Convention on Climate Change, committing countries to reducing greenhouse gas emissions and admitting that global warming exists and is human-made. This was a small first step due to the scientific consensus rapidly forming about climate change.

Another predecessor to ACCCE, the aforementioned Western Fuels Association (WFA), which had a similar makeup with its inception and funding by coal-producing powers, was looking to shift the consensus from global warming as fact to global warming as theory. It all came down to a seed of doubt and an economic message. WFA conducted its own astroturfing of sorts in its trailblazing pro-coal agenda with a front group, the Greening Earth Society. With a name not short on irony, they advocated for increased CO_2 emissions by saying it would help humanity by serving as an "aerial fertilizer" and even saying global warming may just be a good thing for all of us here on the blue planet. The group's founder, Fred Palmer, had a truly mind-boggling quote cited in the *Nation*: "Every time you turn your car on and you burn fossil fuels and you put CO_2 into the air, you're doing the work of the Lord."[29]

This effort between Greening Earth, Western Fuels, and the Center for Energy and Economic Development (CEED), which fought the Kyoto Protocol, was founded by future ACCCE President Steve Miller. At the time, he was a top aide to Kentucky Governor Brereton Jones.

In what would not be the only instance of the United States being the world's foremost leader in special interests, the Senate unanimously opposed the Kyoto Protocol in 1997, thus leaving the United States on its own in the overlap between industrialized nation and climate change denier. Eventually those groups shifted their efforts from opposition to offense with the creation of Americans for Balanced Energy Choices as the start of a proactive approach centered around clean coal.

The years of George W. Bush's presidency provided ease and acceptance to their cause with the Clean Air Act being chopped to bits, standards for mining being lowered, and coal lobbyists swarming all over the administration.

The 2006 midterm elections were good to the Democrats and scary foreshadowing for the coal cronies. The following year, fifty-nine new coal plants were either put on hold or rejected after only twelve had been built in the previous sixteen years. That, and shifting public perception, was the impetus for the two acronyms, CEED and ABEC, to join as one as the ACCCE in 2008 with a message they could rally around that didn't deny climate change, but instead advocated that clean coal could fix the problem.

Those efforts, as described in the *Nation*, entailed "show[ing] up early and often, recruiting a 'grassroots army' of staffers in bright blue T-shirts to trail the candidates, passing out promotional materials at every stop, co-sponsoring presidential debates and running ads in key swing states. The group spent $2 million at the 2008 Democratic convention alone. At a moment of soaring gas prices and deep economic insecurity, ACCCE conveyed a series of easily digestible talking points: 50 percent of the nation's electricity comes from coal; coal is 77 percent cleaner (when you don't include CO_2 emissions) now compared with 1970; America is the Saudi Arabia of coal; coal is cheap, plentiful and clean."[30]

"There absolutely has been a change in message," ACCCE chief spokesman Joe Lucas admitted in the *Nation*. "It's a pro-technology message."[31]

Even with a less combative message, many of the tactics were inherited. Even personnel remained the same. Ned Leonard went from Western Fuels to CEED to ACCCE. Their new, friendlier message wasn't as innocent as it appeared. They opposed the Lieberman-Warner bill and, rather than solely going negative as they had in the past, they instead advocated for separate legislation in the Dingell-Boucher bill, named for Representatives John

Dingell of Detroit and Rick Boucher of southwestern Virginia. They chose to support this version with its various friendly provisions including cost containment measures and rip-offsets. The loopholes were plenty and targets meaningless, so despite more positive messaging the goals were just as insidious: keep burning regardless of science.

The Dingell-Boucher bill, that bill that ACCCE could so generously stomach, was the foundation for their worst nightmare when, in 2008, Henry Waxman of California and Ed Markey of Massachusetts replaced Dingell as chair of the House Energy and Commerce Committee and Boucher as chair of the Subcommittee on Energy and Environment, respectively.

"The analogy I like to use is that it's like being on a boat in the middle of the ocean," Lucas said in the *Nation*. "If you're going 100 knots due north and you're on a big boat and you try and immediately go 100 knots due south, you're going to wreck that boat . . . It's very easy but not too practical to sit there and say, 'Coal will go away,' when we all know that coal is not going to go away. It's going to grow here in America, and even if it were to go away here in America, it's going to grow exponentially in other parts of the world."[32]

Much of the writing was on the wall, but coal wasn't going down without a fight. As Ari Berman put it in the *Nation*: "If Congress and the Obama administration are serious about treating global warming as a pressing economic and ecological threat, coal will struggle to remain relevant. If it hopes to do so, the industry must follow its ads with tangible actions. Nothing less than its survival is at stake"[33]

In September 2009, one of the largest members of ACCCE, Duke Energy, left the coalition. Their stated reasoning was the coalition's opposition to Obama's clean energy agenda. Duke had been among the more global warming–conscious companies despite supporting and being involved in the lobbying efforts.

As characterized in *ThinkProgress*, "ACCCE, in addition to promoting 'clean coal' Christmas carols, employs right-wing public relations firms to paint the American Clean Energy and Security Act as a job-killing energy tax through whatever means necessary—even blatant forgery."[34]

Duke cut ties with ACCCE and, according to the company, the reasoning was "influential member companies who will not support passing climate change legislation in 2009 or 2010." The story in *ThinkProgress* put in context that this was part of a larger battle: "In the meantime, business coalitions like the National Association of Manufacturers, ACCCE, the U.S. Chamber of Commerce, and the American Petroleum Institute (API) are running Astroturf campaigns to kill clean energy legislation."[35]

Merely a week later, Alstom Power joined Duke Energy in its exodus, and later in the year, Alcoa and First Energy followed suit. Without clear reasoning, original members Express Marine and the Western Farmers Electric Cooperative also were no longer listed as members at the end of 2009.

Later that year, *Mother Jones* magazine gave the ACCCE the distinct honor as number three on their list of the "12 loudest members of the chorus claiming that global warming is a joke and that CO_2 emissions are actually good for you."[36]

Mother Jones also chronicled ACCCE's lesser-known efforts at deceptive grassroots lobbying. They had "hired the Lincoln Strategy Group to pack town hall meetings with volunteers from America's Power Army, an organizing group that claims 225,000 warm bodies at its disposal."[37] Lincoln Strategies has a history complete with investigations of destroying Democratic voter registrations in 2004, being banned from Wal-Marts in the state of Tennessee, and organizing a deceptive petition drive against election laws in Arizona.

The author of the *Mother Jones* piece, Josh Harkinson, didn't appreciate the excuses either: "Hauled before Congress last month to explain ACCCE's behavior, CEO Steve Miller claimed that his group had never opposed

Waxman-Markey. That absurd claim led a Democratic congressional spokesman to say he wouldn't rule out referring the matter to the Justice Department for a perjury investigation."[38]

All of this spelled bad days ahead for the twenty-two-year-old ACCCE. In 2015, they had to lay off their chief of staff and eliminate several middle-management positions while looking for options to break a lease for an office downtown in the capital.

"Like many of our members, we are facing tough times that necessitate tough decisions on how best to effectively operate," the group's new CEO, Michael Duncan, a former chairman of the Republican National Committee, said in a statement to *Politico*.[39] The staff was reduced to eight "senior leaders," and that downsizing was spun much the same way clean coal was sold.

"While leaner, this team will continue to execute strategic advocacy efforts ensuring that affordable, reliable coal-based electricity supplies America's power for generations to come," Duncan said in *Politico*.[40]

ACCCE's "lobbying efforts, which peaked during a national advertising blitz in the 2008 presidential campaign when both party's nominees—Barack Obama and John McCain—supported measures to boost 'clean coal' technologies . . . Membership in ACCCE during its heyday included some of the country's largest electric utility companies, as well as coal producers and railroads. But several of those power suppliers, including Mid-American, DTE, Duke and First Energy, have dropped out of the group. And while Southern Company and American Electric Power still have memberships, its roster now is mostly made up of coal and railroad companies that have struggled with slumping stock share prices, bankruptcies and other financial pressure."[41]

CHAPTER 8
MERCER INCORPORATED (THE ALT-RIGHT RENAISSANCE)

The alt-right had cause for celebration in 2016. The fringe movement was stepping out of the shadows, out of the message boards, out of Reddit and hashtags on Twitter. And it was all thanks to Republican presidential candidate Donald Trump, the first politician representing their outside-the-mainstream point of view.

In a *Mother Jones* story about a press conference held by leaders of the movement, titled: "Alt-Right Movement Presents Its Vision for an All-White Society With Trump Paving the Way," Pema Levy laid out the early warning signs of an element of society that would become more prevalent in the years to come:

> The once-fringe movement has suddenly found a prominent place in the Trump campaign and among its most loyal backers. Stephen Bannon, the Trump campaign CEO, was until recently the head of the conservative website Breitbart News, which he called "the platform for the alt-right."[1]

Bannon was the master of ceremonies for the nationalist movement. A month prior to the press conference cited in the article, in early September 2016, the plausible deniability of the connections between the alt-right and

Trump's campaign fell away as Trump appointed Bannon chief executive officer of his campaign at a time when it was looking unlikely he would triumph at the ballot box.

Emily Jane Fox described the decision in *Vanity Fair* as a "double down on some of the Trump's campaigns most fringe elements."[2]

The decision was not made in a vacuum; it was made by the financier of the alt-right, the gardener who planted the astroturf that Bannon maintained. Robert Mercer, and his daughter Rebekah, had supported the Trump campaign since Ted Cruz's chances became obsolete. They supported Trump, and Bannon was their guy. Fox wrote:

> By the time Cruz refused to endorse Trump onstage at the Republican National Convention, the notoriously private family released a statement in support of the billionaire developer that concluded, "We need all hands on deck to ensure that Mr. Trump prevails." For the Mercers, that apparently included bringing Bannon on board . . . The Mercers' ties to Bannon run deep. According to Bloomberg, the family first invested $10 million in Breitbart News in 2011.[3]

Robert Mercer was not new to politics. Trump, the man he funded to new heights of influence, was, and Mercer exploited that fact to run a campaign rallying together a silent majority known as the alt-right, but accused by many of being no more than bigoted white supremacists—anti-Semitic neo-Nazis. Trump's appeal alluded political reporters who had covered successful and unsuccessful campaigns alike. His rabid following cherished the idea of an outsider brought in to shake things up and, crowds chanted at his campaign rallies (which felt more like pep rallies) to "Drain the Swamp!" of lifelong politicians, special interest groups, lobbyists, and politicians indebted to the moneyed interests that funded and sustained their public sector careers.

Yet, Trump's boasts of being an outsider and the so-called alt-rights' claims of being neglected by the majority were unrealistic.

Mercer made his money in finance, specifically by developing algorithmic trading strategies and artificial intelligence and implementing them while serving as the co-chief executive officer at hedge fund Renaissance Technologies.

The political activities of the seventy-year-old financial titan laid the groundwork for Trump's base that would eventually be the loyal parishioners of Trumpism. In conjunction with Patrick Caddell, a former Democratic political consultant who worked in the White House with Jimmy Carter, Mercer conducted political testing and research into popular opinion. Mercer and Caddell's work found that, as reported by Jane Mayer in the *New Yorker*, political conditions in America were increasingly ripe for an outsider candidate to take the White House. Caddell is quoted in the story describing the financier as a libertarian who "despises the Republican establishment" and "thinks that the leaders are corrupt crooks, and that they've ruined the country."[4]

Another part of that equation, the mastermind who laid the astroturf on which Trump claimed grassroots support, was Steve Bannon. Bannon was the one identified by the media and opposition as the architect from which the most isolationist, anarchist, and white supremacist ideas espoused by Trump were originating. However, Bannon had not achieved this on his own; he was in many ways a creation of the Mercer political machine.

In February 2017, Trump tweeted "The FAKE NEWS media (failing @nytimes, @NBCNews, @ABC, @CBS, @CNN) is not my enemy, it is the enemy of the American People!"[5] A few years earlier in 2012, Caddell had referred to the media as "the enemy of the American people"[6] in a speech at a conference put together by a conservative group, Accuracy in Media. At the time, the machine that would eventually propel Trump to 1600 Pennsylvania Avenue was being finely tuned. That speech was covered on a little-known website, Breitbart News. That site's executive chairman was, with a brief break to run a campaign and serve an abnormally short tenure in the Executive Branch, Steve Bannon. Bannon stepped down as chairman in January 2017 as his opportunity to work on his agenda at the White House seemed more productive than at the blog. One of the site's major stakeholders is Robert Mercer.

The money for that stake in a budding fringe news site came from Mercer's work at Renaissance. Dubbed a "computer genius," Mercer has never been public about his politics or political efforts. As of late it has been harder for him to avoid attention, since he has become a well-known name in political circles.

"I have no idea what his political views are—they're unknown, not just to the public but also to most people who've been active in politics for the past thirty years," Trevor Potter, former chairman of the Federal Election Commission, told the *New Yorker's* Jane Mayer.[7]

Whatever ideas may be held of Mercer, it is a rarity to hear him come out publicly to either affirm or denounce those impressions. In a 2010 *Wall Street Journal* piece about Mercer running Renaissance, he responded with a statement saying in part, "I'm happy going through my life without saying anything to anybody."[8]

That sets him apart from the mega-lobbyists and astroturfing kingpins with whom he would be compared. But what most definitely is a unifying factor between Mercer and the Kochs of the world is that the *Citizens United v. Federal Election Commission* Supreme Court case, which expanded the rights and freedoms around political donations, opened up a new world of possibilities for their subversive work. That case is well known for being the lynchpin moment where mega-donors became the most important members of the political class. It was a case that was integral to Mercer's efforts.

Potter spoke ominously of that case, telling Mayer, "a single billionaire can write an eight-figure check and put not just their thumb but their whole hand on the scale—and we often have no idea who they are. Suddenly, a random billionaire can change politics and public policy—to sweep everything else off the table—even if they don't speak publicly, and even if there's almost no public awareness of his or her views."[9]

While being quiet in front of a microphone or recorder, Mercer speaks loudly with his wallet. As he attempts to mold the Republican party, and—with their stranglehold on the government—the country to his beliefs, there has been some cause for concern.

As the president was settling into his new residence, a member of the senior staff at Renaissance, David Magerman, voiced his concerns for the movement that had grown from the seeds planted by Mercer's checkbook. A Democrat concerned with rising anti-Semitism, Magerman first had a verbal spat with his boss, according to Mayer's reporting, but after a thirty-day suspension and accounts of the internal strife in the *Wall Street Journal*, Magerman took his dissent to the op-ed pages of the *Philadelphia Inquirer*.

"Robert Mercer, the co-CEO of Renaissance Technologies and my boss's boss, holds views with which I disagree and, in some cases, find abhorrent," wrote Magerman, describing Mercer's eventual donations to Trump after Cruz dropped out as "buying shares in the candidate, and Robert Mercer now owns a sizeable share of the United States Presidency."[10]

Magerman pointed to the web of connections including Mercer's Breitbart ownership, connections with campaign manager and counselor Kellyanne Conway and Steve Bannon as well as Rebekah Mercer's position on the transition team as evidence of how ingrained in the administration this donor, his boss, was.

"Mercer also has insisted that Trump use his company Cambridge Analytica, which uses its statistical models of voter psychology to get unpopular initiatives (like electing Donald Trump) through the electorate," Magerman continued. "Mercer has surrounded our President with his people, and his people have an outsized influence over the running of our country, simply because Robert Mercer paid for their seats."[11]

If those sentiments weren't blunt enough, a former Renaissance employee, Nick Patterson, told Mayer, "He's not the first person in history to use money in politics, but in my view Trump wouldn't be President if not for Bob. It doesn't get much more effective than that."[12]

Patterson told Mayer that Mercer has a "susceptibility to conspiracy theories about Bill and Hillary Clinton."[13] The same story details his stance that the impact of climate change was exaggerated, that the United States should have taken oil from Iraq during the Persian Gulf War, and that the Civil Rights Act of 1964 was a mistake. All of these sentiments have been echoed by Trump or those who surrounded him in the campaign and now the administration. There were also, like his heirs apparent the Kochs, libertarian and fiscally conservative views present, and some former employees described it as objectivism, the belief system stemming from Ayn Rand's *Atlas Shrugged*.

Trump was not a natural fit with Mercer, nor was Mercer with many conservatives or ideologues who were confounded by Trump's seeming lack of ideology. That being said, he had a vehement and deep-seated hatred of Hillary Clinton and thought a disrupter of the two parties he disdained and the large government he held in contempt was a worthy cause.

Surely the likes of Bannon, Conway, and Rebekah Mercer helped bridge the gap between Mercer's money and the "Make America Great Again" ethos. However, his mathematical background led him to look for a way to increase the odds that he would receive a return on investment from his support of Trump. At the time, the polls and the gaffes didn't bode well for his chances.

Mercer's donations surpassed most political donors. At $22.5 million in disclosed donations to Republicans and political action committees, his efforts go beyond throwing money at campaigns and instead contain the important astroturfing efforts necessary to build a movement.

Mercer's political machine is a complex web, with the Mercer Family Foundation at the center. Originally founded for medical research and charity when established in 2004, by 2008, Rebekah, by many accounts the political and conservative impetus within the bloodstream, had transformed it into a political force funding attacks on Hillary Clinton. That trend continued through 2015 when the foundation held $24.5 million and awarded large sums to conservative organizations on a regular basis.

Unlike other donors who have risen to the level of astroturfing, the Mercers have employed private industry in their aggressive actions. Breitbart News, the epicenter of the alt-right, was given $10 million to be a right-wing mirror image of the Huffington Post and many believe has gone further to the pole than even Arianna Huffington's namesake. With a mixture of conservative orthodoxy and dog whistle racism, the site named for Andrew Breitbart and run by friend-of-the-family Bannon had its greatest operation to date in using their 19.2 million unique visitors a month to attack and destroy Hillary Clinton and her bid for the White House. There are too many variables to be sure, but no story about how Trump was triumphant against nearly insurmountable odds is complete without mention of the site. However, that was not the only tool in Mercer's arsenal, or portfolio, integral to Trump's triumph.

Cambridge Analytica, a data mining and research firm, is a project right in Mercer's wheelhouse. Claiming to use psychology in their unique analysis of voting trends and individual voters, they look to decipher the ideal messaging to change hearts and minds. A subsidiary of London-based Strategic Communication Laboratories, the firm worked with Trump, as well as on the Brexit campaign, which resulted in Great Britain's citizens voting to leave the European Union.

The importance of these instruments in the November 2016 election results is up for debate, but some believe it was even more instrumental than Breitbart, which is often cited as an important persuasive propaganda arm of the Trump campaign. Breitbart, of course, has an air of legitimacy of not being seen as messaging "directly from the campaign," but often nevertheless falling in lockstep with whatever message the campaign—now administration—would want.

Jonathan Albright, an assistant professor of Communications at Elon University in North Carolina, recently published a paper, on *Medium*, calling Cambridge Analytica a "propaganda machine."

As part of his efforts, Mercer does have surrogates and delegates much the way a politician does. Before Trump, Mercer was working with Bannon who, since as early as 2012, was a middleman between Mercer and the political world. There is some chicken and egg, horse and cart type debates over whether Bannon is Mercer's pawn or Mercer is Bannon's inept financier. As Mayer wrote:

> Some people who have observed the Mercers' political evolution worry that Bannon has become a Svengali to the whole family, exploiting its political inexperience and tapping its fortune to further his own ambitions. It was Bannon who urged the Mercers to invest in a data-analytics firm. He also encouraged the investment in Breitbart News, which was made through Gravitas Maximus, L.L.C., a front group that once had the same Long Island address as Renaissance Technologies. In an interview, Bannon praised the Mercers' strategic approach: "The Mercers laid the groundwork for the Trump revolution. Irrefutably, when you look at donors during the past four years, they have had the single biggest impact of anybody, including the Kochs."[14]

Bannon and other parts of Mercer incorporated came to the aid of a vulnerable Trump campaign looking dead on arrival in summer 2016. A claim could be made that Mercer took over the campaign at the brink of failure and guided it to victory.

The elder Mercer's political leanings were rarely, if ever, on public display, owing to his preference for privacy. In a 2014 speech following being awarded a lifetime-achievement award from the Association for Computational Linguistics, Mercer bemoaned that government was made to consume, and colleagues told Mayer that he believes the government is inefficient. His preference for self-sufficiency had exceptions bordering on hypocrisy when he faced a lack of funding for a project at his job prior to Renaissance. His IBM project focusing on translation was underfunded and he got additional funding from a Pentagon program. This funding from the public sector he disdained was integral to his early career success.

However, when it came to funding the government that had funded him, Renaissance's fulfillment of tax obligations has been questionable. A 2014 Senate inquiry found that they had incorrectly classified short-term trades as long term to the tune of $6.8 million in taxes evaded.[15] Despite no criminal allegations, the Internal Revenue Service (IRS) demanded payment and described the actions as abusive; the issue now stands in front of the current government led by Mercer's man. It is unclear how it will shake out, but it's a textbook case of why the wealthy make these types of donations, or "investments."

While Robert Mercer may have started the family's involvement in politics. Rebekah has stepped into the political sphere more firmly and wholeheartedly than her father ever has.

After attending college at Stanford University, she worked at Renaissance with her father. After getting married she bought six apartments and combined them to create one massive domicile at Trump Place on the Upper West Side of Manhattan. Mayer described her recent foray into the political world by saying, "in recent years she has become consumed by politics,"[16] before quoting Christopher Ruddy, the owner of Newsmax Media as saying, "She is the First Lady of the alt-right . . . She's respected in conservative circles, and clearly Trump has embraced her in a big way."[17]

The Mercers' first foray into astroturfing began in 2010, not so coincidentally after the *Citizens United* ruling. They used that as impetus to try their hand in tipping the scales first in an effort to fight the building of a Muslim cultural center near the site of the former World Trade Center in Manhattan with a campaign claiming, incorrectly, that it would be a "ground zero mosque."[18] Using Islamophobia and through donations to an Oregon-based super PAC aimed to help a New York gubernatorial candidate with similar views, they were ultimately unsuccessful in the liberal, diverse, open-minded city. Nonetheless, the cultural center was never built and reporters in New York eventually found that Mercer was the sole donor behind the smear campaign.

It was also in Oregon where the Mercers gave $640,000 to a group that stood against Democratic Representative Peter DeFazio, using negative ads in a lead up to his 2010 bid for reelection. Robert Mercer clearly held a preference for those right of center, but Arthur Robinson, who Oregon senator Jeff Merkley once called an "extremist kook"[19] was running against DeFazio. Robinson is among those on the Mercer's balance sheet, being the recipient of at least $1.6 million in donations through his Oregon Institute of Science and Medicine. But the Mercers also failed in this effort with DeFazio calling out the Wall Street special interests attempting to meddle in the Beaver State.

At the end of their first election cycle in the lobbying game, they were winless with losses in New York and Oregon despite a wave year for Republicans. These were poor returns on investment for someone who made a career managing just that at a statistical level.

The following year the Mercers worked with the Kochs, attending their seminars set up to help other right-wing donors effectively use their funds. They started in that incubator giving money to a fund the Kochs ran, pooling money and doling it out effectively across the nation where needed. Mayer estimated their introductory contribution at a generous million annually to the fund and getting up to more than $25 million overall.

Making moves closer to the inside and closer to DC, they joined the Council for National Policy, described in the pages of the *New York Times* as a "little-known club of a few hundred of the most powerful conservatives in the country."[20] That is where they found fellow Clinton conspiracy theorists, as well as Steve Bannon and Kellyanne Conway.

In 2011, they met Andrew Breitbart and, impressed with his mission, donated and met Bannon who, at the time, housed the online publication in a Santa Monica office space he owned. Bannon had gotten to that spot by way of Harvard Business School, Goldman Sachs, and a foray into political films.

In 2011, the first plan and strategy took form with Bannon putting together a business plan for the rich donors featuring $10 million to Breitbart, thus taking a large stake in the company, and placing Bannon on the board of directors. When Andrew Breitbart died the following year, Bannon became the executive chairman and the Mercers his backer. Bannon's stewardship at Breitbart led to the explosion of the platform, including hiring a group of full-time writers and steering the ship to parts of the conservative caucus that were considered undesirable due to white nationalism, sexism, and racism. Among those writers given a platform was the incendiary Milo Yiannopoulos.

The site was increasing in pervasiveness and gearing up, knowingly or unknowingly, for its foray into the White House. Two years later, when the alt-right had a presidential candidate, Breitbart claimed to have the most shared political content on Facebook. This was how the most conservative the country had to offer—what was previously the underbelly of the Republican Party—came to mainstream success. It also gave the Mercers unmatched power integral to their astroturfing.

"'She reads every story, and calls when there are grammatical errors or typos." Though she doesn't dictate a political line to the editors, she often points out areas of coverage that she thinks require more attention. Her views about the Washington establishment, including the Republican leadership, are scathing. "She was at the avant-garde of shuttering both political parties,"[21] a Breitbart insider told Mayer of Rebekah Mercer.

They used their platform to promote those elements of the conservative movement that were antiestablishment and unable to get a strong foothold, billed as the "silent majority" and rallied as unnoticed by the "mainstream media."

While this renaissance was underway in the alt-right machine, which was reaching heights previously unseen, their figurehead was being cultivated. In 2011, David Bossie of Citizens United introduced Donald Trump and Steve Bannon. Trump was debating a campaign against Barack Obama.

They first met at Trump Tower, where four years later Trump would ride down the escalator to announce a candidacy at the time regarded as a joke. At the time, in 2012, running was not the move for Trump, but a relationship was forged and Breitbart covered Trump in a positive light going forward. As Mayer detailed: "Bannon noticed that, when Trump spoke to crowds, people were electrified. Bannon began to think that Trump might be 'the one' who could shake up American politics."[22]

That meeting with Bannon and subsequent coverage in Breitbart gave Trump an early constituency and, though the masses viewed it with skepticism, an added degree of legitimacy in the political arena. That, of course, was also of huge value when Trump burst onto the political scene with his birtherism movement (where he raised the question of whether President Obama had been born in the United States). That pivoted to knocks on the establishment on both sides of the aisle, a strategy that worked for Trump and the Breitbart crowd.

Subsequently, the Mercer Family Foundation was expanding with $11 million headed to the Media Research Center and their anti-mainstream media mission. Their mission, according to their site, is to "expose and neutralize the propaganda arm of the Left: the national news media."[23] Thus, a key platform of Trump's campaign was already being pushed. There was also a donation to Citizens United that forced the release of the emails that followed Clinton through the 2016 election through a Freedom of Information Act request funded by a $550,000 Mercer check, which would ultimately be the impetus for the opening of Pandora's box of political donations. The Supreme Court case would give the Mercer's the ability to astroturf an alt-right movement that marched all the way to the White House steps.

The Mercers' web was forming through the interconnectivity of their donations and subordinates. In 2012, a foundation run by Citizens United paid Bannon's consulting group Bannon Strategic Advisors $300,000 for fundraising services.

An early Caddell-Bannon-Bossie joint effort sponsored by Mercer was the creation of films smearing President Obama during his run for reelection. Not so coincidentally, Rebekah Mercer sits on the board of a conservative group that aims to oppose and compete with Hollywood liberalism by creating its own entertainment. Obama was too strong a force to take down, but the practice run would come in handy when a stronger demagogue and weaker Democrat replaced Romney and Obama as the lead characters. That, and the fact that Rebekah Mercer stepped off the sidelines.

"Obama's defeat of Mitt Romney particularly infuriated Rebekah Mercer, who concluded that the pollsters, the data crunchers, and the spin doctors were all frauds. Soon afterward, Republican Party officials invited big donors to the University Club, in New York, for a postmortem on the election," wrote Mayer. "Attendees were stunned when Rebekah Mercer 'ripped the shit out of them,' a friend of hers told me, adding, 'It was really her coming out.' As the *Financial Times* has reported, from that point on Mercer wanted to know exactly how her donations were being spent and wanted to invest only in what another friend described as 'things that she thinks put lead on the target.'"[24]

The web of affiliations continued to grow over the years, a sign of a maturing manufactured movement. Bannon founded the Government Accountability Institute and Rebekah sat on the board; her family foundation gave at least a million dollars annually from 2013–15. It was billed as a nonpartisan research institute. But the truth was not hard to find, since in 2015 Bannon told *Bloomberg Businessweek* that the real goal was to dig up dirt on politicians and feed it to the mainstream media.[25]

They aimed to get information in unsavory ways and feed it to the mainstream media who had been short-staffed and shortchanged by industry cut backs. An example of their success came in April 2015 with a front-page story in the *New York Times* based on a book by Peter Schweizer, president of the Government Accountability Institute, titled *Clinton Cash*. With the establishment in their crosshairs, this anarchic movement wasn't partisan: they followed up with another controversial release in *Bush Bucks*, about Jeb Bush who stood as a formidable force between the alt-right and the executive branch.

Along with the growing of the Mercer network, the aspiring operatives continued standard lobbying protocol by giving money to campaigns. However, they did it through the professionals. The Kochs' Freedom Partners Action Fund received $2.5 million in 2014, a notable moment when they contributed more than the namesakes that was marked by the Bloomberg News headline: "The Man who out-Koched the Kochs."[26]

A harbinger of things to come, Rebekah was reportedly "over" the Kochs and their failure to stop Obama. When that frustration led her to branch out on her own, she was convincing enough to prompt other donors to make the same move.

Out of those ashes came Cambridge Analytica as a response to Democrats being more advanced in the art of digital analytics. It was a natural extension for a person who had revolutionized data use in finance. Cambridge Analytica shares an address in Manhattan with the Rebekah Mercer–chaired Reclaim New York: a group that opposes government spending. Steve Bannon served as a corporate officer at both.

The importance Cambridge played in 2016 is debated and unclear, but it is as good a suspect as any for the reason Trump was triumphant. A small subset of very demographically advantageous voters were somehow swayed from undecided to red in swing states nationwide, prompting a swing state sweep and underdog victory. This work and the success of the Trump campaign remains up in the air as a potentially criminal matter depending on the findings of Special Counsel Robert Mueller.

Other data-driven objectives have been sponsored by Mercer Co. Perhaps the most integral was a poll conducted by Caddell and shown to the Mercers in 2013 that had results so incredulous, Mercer ordered them redone. However, both versions showed the same thing: Americans were increasingly spiteful of wealthy elites who they were convinced corrupted government to only help themselves. And a handful of wealthy elites was going to exploit that sentiment with a faux-populist astroturfing campaign.

In the run up to one of the most improbable election days in United States history, Mercer paid Caddell to continue the analytical work on polling that showed a distaste for the elites. The fact that they themselves were elites seemed to be easily ignorable not only for the lobbyists, but, as would be evidenced in November 2016, for the electorate. The effort started with Caddell hoping to push for support of a third-party candidate as the anti-establishment trend became more and more pronounced through the lead up to votes being cast. As it became clear that a literal third-party candidate, as in representing a party that isn't the Democrats or Republicans, was not in the cards, the next best thing was plotted. With the two campaigns running, it was obvious with their political leanings that Trump was the best horse to back if the evidence of voter distaste for political elites was to be acted upon.

This was not an immediate action or instinct from the man with the money, however. Mercer went through the primaries and at first was supportive of Cruz, who had tried to use the outsider label due to his colleagues' dislike of him and his insistence on shutting down the government a few years prior. Eleven million dollars made the Cruz campaign Mercer-sponsored, but according to reporting by *Politico*, Rebekah was not well-liked within the campaign because of the opinions and hands-on approach that came along with the money. After Cruz was dispatched by Trump, the Mercers put their support behind Trump. According to a Mercer quote that appeared in the *New York Times*, Mercer may have been more against Clinton than for any candidate, levying the conspiratorial and paranoid claim that a Clinton presidency would lead to the "repeal [of] both the First and Second Amendments of the Bill of Rights."[27]

The incestuous nature of this political machine was evidenced by Kellyanne Conway jumping ship for greener pastures after Cruz was no longer a viable candidate, much like the wealthy donors. The Mercer's super PAC was redirected from Cruz to Trump and another two million dollars was added for good measure. Mayer even saw evidence of a tradeoff for that over the top donation that led to the hiring of Cambridge Analytica out of deference to the Mercers. Little did the Trump folks know, it would be a key cog in their victory.

When Paul Manafort was forced to resign as Trump's campaign manager upon revelations of his shady connections in Russia and Ukraine, there was a void left in the power structure of the campaign. The Mercers inserted themselves and got the astroturf in full gear. Rebekah was the main conduit to the campaign from the Mercers, and she had garnered a reputation for moving up her people to principal positions. Bannon became the campaign CEO, Conway became the campaign manager, and Bossie the deputy campaign manager.

Weekly Standard editor and vocal Trump critic William Kristol characterized the moves as a "merger of the Trump campaign with the kooky right."[28]

A leaked email obtained by the *New Yorker* made the appointments even more nefarious as it seemed the Mercer machine had control over the campaign prior to it being formalized. The email featured Bannon calling himself the de facto campaign manager and talking about Breitbart's pro-Trump coverage, which had been paid for by the Mercers and was a key cog in the Trump machine.

Mayer discussed just how dangerous this form of astroturfing, so directly linked to a presidential campaign, was, in no uncertain terms:

Brendan Fischer, a lawyer at the Campaign Legal Center, said that the Mercers' financial entanglement with the Trump campaign was "bizarre" and potentially "illegal." The group has filed a complaint with the Federal Election Commission, which notes that, at the end of the 2016 campaign, the super PAC run by the Mercers paid Glittering Steel—a film-production company that shares an address in Los Angeles with Cambridge Analytica and Breitbart News—two hundred and eighty thousand dollars, supposedly for campaign ads attacking Hillary Clinton. Although Bannon was running Trump's campaign, Fischer said that it appears to have paid him nothing. Meanwhile, the Mercers' super PAC made a payment of about five million dollars to Cambridge Analytica, which was incorporated at the same address as Bannon Strategic Advisors. Super PACs are legally required to stay independent of a candidate's campaign. But, Fischer said, "it raises the possibility of the Mercers subsidizing Steve Bannon's work for the Trump campaign."[29]

After their mission was accomplished, the Mercers held a victory party with many of their soldiers in attendance, including the front man, then-president-elect Donald Trump. Trump spoke at the event, saying the Mercers were "instrumental in bringing some organization," according to Mayer.

Rebekah would serve on the transition team with Fischer, who told Mayer, "She basically bought herself a seat."[30]

She continued to have a massive influence over the administration, both hitting and missing on her suggestions, of which there were no shortage. She wasn't immediately able to get jobs for her allies John Bolton and Arthur Robinson (though Bolton would eventually replace General James Mattis as National Security Adviser in April 2018) but was an advocate behind the hiring of Michael Flynn, Steve Bannon, and Kellyanne Conway. Of course, two of those three did not work out as planned (with Flynn resigning in disgrace after only twenty-four days and Bannon after seven months). Yet, whichever way you slice it, Mercer's influence was and remains inseparable from the actions of the Trump presidency.

Due to the electoral college victory for Mercer's preferred candidate and the mainstreaming of the cause he had championed and built, Mercer received the attention he had tried so hard to avoid. With that came a reckoning, not only for his own actions but also for the actions of those his wallet had empowered. Having donated $24.6 million to Republicans in 2016, and more importantly, been quick to support Trump and bankroll Breitbart, the nation blamed him for the failures of the administration.

The dissent was not limited to those removed from his sphere of influence. As Alana Abramson and Lucinda Shen wrote in *Fortune*, "Mercer's backing of Breitbart News, Bannon, and Trump have put him at odds with Renaissance Technologies' leadership. Like many financial bigwigs, Renaissance founder and chairman James Simons backed Democratic Party nominee Hillary Clinton during the 2016 elections. Mercer, on the other hand, gave at least $15 million to a PAC dubbed Make America Number 1—an organization that backed Trump."[31]

In a letter dated November 2, 2017, nearly a year after the election, Mercer wrote to his colleagues at Renaissance Technologies announcing his resignation as CEO and also distancing himself from controversy over his political ties to associates of President Trump, according to Bloomberg, which went on to detail exactly why Mercer had been spooked.

"In recent months, Mercer's personal political projects dragged the notoriously secretive firm into the national spotlight," Janet Lorin and Katherin Burton wrote in *Bloomberg Businessweek*. "Mercer and his daughter, Rebekah, are prominent Republican donors and patrons of Stephen Bannon, the chairman of Breitbart News and a driving force behind the populist, nationalist wing of the Republican Party that carried Trump to the White House."[32]

The letter itself directly addressed the allegations and heat he had received as it became more and more clear he was the gardener of the astroturf: "During the past year, I have been the object of a great deal of scrutiny from the press,"[33] wrote Mercer, adding that he aimed to "correct some of the misinformation that has been published about me." He characterized his support for Republicans as innocuous and solely a demonstration of his preference for "a smaller, less powerful government."[34] Don't *most* people who favor a small government set up organizations to fuel a populist candidate and to publish propaganda on his behalf?

He directly tackled the attacks on the prejudice he had funded and surprisingly made mention of Bannon, the embodiment of his bad reputation:

> Of the many mischaracterizations made of me by the press, the most repugnant to me have been the intimations that I am a white supremacist or a member of some other noxious group. Discrimination on the basis of race, ethnicity, gender, creed, or anything of that sort is abhorrent to me. But more than that, it is ignorant. The press has also intimated that my politics marches in lockstep with Steve Bannon's. I have great respect for Mr. Bannon, and from time to time I do discuss politics with him. However, I make my own decisions with respect to whom I support politically. Those decisions do not always align with Mr. Bannon's.[35]

This reckoning also featured Bannon disciple Milo Yiannopoulos, whom Mercer supported "in the hope and expectation that his expression of views contrary to the social mainstream . . . would promote the type of open debate and freedom of thought that is being throttled."[36] An article from

Buzzfeed highlighting Yiannopoulos's footsie with Nazis and Nazism forced the hand of the recluse; he had to say something: "Actions of and statements by Mr. Yiannopoulos have caused pain and divisiveness undermining the open and productive discourse that I had hoped to facilitate. I was mistaken to have supported him, and for several weeks have been in the process of severing all ties with him. For personal reasons, I have also decided to sell my stake in Breitbart News to my daughters."[37]

CNN Money wrote that the continuation of the mission through Rebekah "suggests not much may immediately change at the right-wing website. His daughter Rebekah Mercer is a strong supporter of President Trump and previously served on the executive committee for his transition."[38]

That aforementioned strife within Renaissance may have been due to the *Buzzfeed* report. *Buzzfeed* wrote when news broke of the Mercer resignations: "Sources familiar with Renaissance informed BuzzFeed News in recent days of significant anger within the company about the report."[39]

It was notable, as Tina Nguyen noted in *Vanity Fair*, that the denunciation of Bannon was far more ambiguous than that of Yiannopolous. Nguyen wrote:

While Mercer's denunciation of Yiannopoulos left no room for ambiguity, his efforts to distance himself from Bannon were comparatively tempered, leaving open the question of whether the Mercers will continue their association with the populist-nationalist movement. Former Breitbart employees familiar with the Mercers' strategies pointed out that while Bob had publicly distanced himself from Renaissance, he had not divested, and still maintains a sizable fortune. "This seems to me much more like Robert Mercer separating . . . his image from his money-making capacity than an actual disassociation with the people he funded for so long," said Ben Shapiro, the former editor-at-large at Breitbart who broke with the site in 2016. "The only person who's really damaged here is Yiannopoulos. Rebekah's gonna continue funding Breitbart, [and] there's no repentance or shift here . . . it's just a P.R. maneuver to [take] pressure off his hedge-fund investors."[40]

Prior to Mercer's statement, the *Buzzfeed* exposé fueled pressure from the organization Sleeping Giants, a Twitter account highlighting advertisements on the controversial site with the goal of deterring advertising revenue. In addition there was a push for universities and pension funds to divest from Renaissance in direct response to its fueling of Breitbart and the alt-right. The reaction seemed warranted based on the story.

In the Sleeping Giants campaign, they did not mince words about Mercer's involvement in the alt-right. "While Steve Bannon gets much of the spotlight for his inflammatory website Breitbart News, it is the billionaire investor, Robert Mercer, who is responsible for growing the scale and reach the site's racist agenda has today,"[41] the campaign statement read.

This didn't slow down other parts of the Mercer mission, which now extended to numerous sectors and down the ballot. As the *Washington Examiner* wrote, "Mercer was a major donor to President Trump's campaign and has donated millions of dollars to other Republican candidates for lower offices. He's known as a major backer for Kelli Ward, who's running for Senator Jeff Flake's seat in Arizona in 2018."[42] Ward would go on to lose the primary for that seat.

Mercer's connection to Yiannopoulos was not solely through his mentor Bannon; prior to the Mercer letter, Rebekah and Bob were funding Milo Inc., his post-Breitbart media venture.

Even after being thrown off the gravy train, Yiannopoulos seemed to make it clear that despite being a man with reverence for no one and nothing, Mercer was an exception, the reason he had made it so far.

"For his part, the famously outspoken Yiannopoulos avoided responding to Mercer's criticism. 'I am grateful for Bob's help in getting me this far in my career. I wish him and the family all the best,'" wrote *Business Insider*, including the quote his spokesperson gave them.

Rebekah had always been a key cog and seemingly the more politically enthralled of the two.

And in Rebekah could be the continuation of the Mercers' mission, according to *New York* magazine:

> Breitbart News was only part of the vast conservative empire established by Mercer and his daughter Rebekah. His fortune funded PACs, think tanks, lobbying groups, and tech firms, many of which would eventually go to work for Trump . . . When so many wealthy conservative donors were staying away from Trump, the Mercers went all-in, and it's hardly a stretch to suggest that without Robert Mercer, there is no President Trump . . . In the end, though, Mercer's boosting of Trump appears to have cost him his job.[43]

Despite the Mercer disavowal of Milo and, to a lesser extent, Bannon, Rosie Gray wrote with skepticism in the *Atlantic* about the chance that there would be any fundamental change in the power structure of the alt-right and their mission:

> Mercer's comments could seem a bad sign for Bannon, though a Bannon ally said there were no negative implications for the intra-party insurgency against establishment Republicans Bannon is planning for the 2018 midterm elections . . . Another Republican source with knowledge of the situation predicted that "There's gonna be no financial distance at the end of the day." Even before this, Mercer's daughter Rebekah had played a decisive role in the family's political decisions.[44]

This support in the face of adversity to their cause was not a first, as chronicled in the same piece from the *Atlantic*, which detailed how, after the *Access Hollywood* tape that shook the campaign and showed Trump boasting about sexual assault, Robert Mercer defended him while most others were distancing themselves: "They called the comments on the tape 'locker room braggadocio' and slammed 'those among the political elite who quake before the boombox of media blather' who 'do not appreciate the apocalyptic choice that America faces on Nov. 8.'"[45]

The *Buzzfeed* piece that caused so much backlash against the alt-right and forced Mercer to go public in disapproval featured email leaks substantiating a long held suspicion of connections between Breitbart, which maintains plausible deniability about being racist or anti-Semitic, and the openly hateful wings of the alt-right.

Buzzfeed wrote of the leaks that they, "clearly show that Breitbart does more than tolerate the most hate-filled, racist voices of the alt-right. It thrives on them, fueling and being fueled by some of the most toxic beliefs on the political spectrum—and clearing the way for them to enter the American mainstream."[46]

Mercer was not spared by *Buzzfeed*: "These documents chart the Breitbart alt-right universe. They reveal how the website—and, in particular, Yiannopoulos—links the Mercer family, the billionaires who fund Breitbart, to underpaid trolls who fill it with provocative content, and to extremists striving to create a white ethnostate. . . . They capture what Bannon calls his 'killing machine' in action, as it dredges up the resentments of people around the world, sifts through these grievances for ideas and content, and propels them from the unsavory parts of the internet up to TrumpWorld, collecting advertisers' checks all along the way."[47]

With Bannon back at Breitbart by that point, those revelations seemed even more relevant. Among the less desirable connections that were highlighted as part of the astroturfing effort Bannon dubbed as "#war" in the leaked emails, were Andrew "Weev" Auernheimer of the openly neo-Nazi *Daily Stormer*, Curtis Yarvin who has written extensively as part of the "neoreactionary" movement and believes in eugenics, and Devin Saucier who edits the white nationalist magazine *American Renaissance*. Saucier wrote a story in June 2017 titled "Why I Am (Among Other Things) a White Nationalist."[48] These connections are what caused a reckoning for Mercer. Though Yiannopoulos was the point of contact, the emails revealed that the Mercers' errand boy was also involved.

"Bannon, as you probably know, is sympathetic to much of it,"[49] Milo wrote to Saucier.

This correspondence was in relation to a massive alt-right piece that would chart the anatomy of the movement. It is helpful in understanding what corners of the internet Mercer's money was bringing to the mainstream. The ghostwritten story, according to *Buzzfeed*, chronicled, "a taxonomy of the movement titled 'ALT-RIGHT BEHEMOTH.' It included a little bit of everything: the brains and their influences (Yarvin and Evola, etc.), the 'natural conservatives' (people who think different ethnic groups should stay separate for scientific reasons), the 'Meme team' (4chan and 8chan), and the actual hatemongers."[50]

Editors rejected that initial draft and were looking to separate Breitbart a bit more distinctly from neo-Nazis. The need to even have to make that distinction is not ideal.

The piece eventually became "An Establishment Conservative's Guide to the Alt-Right."[51] From there, Joseph Bernstein of *Buzzfeed* lays out that massive impact:

It quickly became a touchstone, cited in the New York Times, the Los Angeles Times, the New Yorker, CNN, and New York Magazine, among others. And its influence is still being felt. This past July, in a speech in Warsaw that was celebrated by the alt-right, President Trump echoed a line from the story—a story written by a "brown-sounding" amanuensis, all but line-edited by a white nationalist, laundered for racism by Breitbart's editors, and supervised by the man who would in short order become the president's chief strategist. The machine had worked well.[52]

Buzzfeed also captured how Rebekah had gotten closer and more intertwined with the movement than her father ever had, even pushing stories to Bannon. In 2016, Mercer emailed Bannon to meet an app developer who had a game in which one deleted emails like Hillary Clinton, and was rejected by the app store. She suggested a story about his "1st amendment political persecution." After Breitbart ran a pair of stories on the app, Apple reversed their decision. "This was the usual way stories came in from the Mercers, according to a former Breitbart editor: with a request from Bannon referring to 'our investors' or 'our investing partners.'"[53]

The worst of it came with revelations in the piece that, at one point, Mercer's private security company was protecting Yiannopoulos as he toured and caused chaos.

As Breitbart was walking a thin line between Nazi and alt-right with emails containing debates about Holocaust jokes, Bannon was receiving his appointment to run the Trump campaign. During that time he was still in correspondence with Breitbart, basically making the alt-right outlet a propaganda machine.

Milo once emailed someone saying that Trump "used phrases extremely close to what I say—Bannon is feeding him."[54] He even looked for an endorsement from Donald Trump Jr. or Ivanka Trump for his book.

The *Buzzfeed* piece concluded: "It was a brilliant audience expansion machine, financed by billionaires, designed to draw in people disgusted by some combination of identity politics, Muslim and Hispanic immigration, and the idea of Hillary Clinton or Barack Obama in the White House.

And if expanding that audience meant involving white nationalists and neo-Nazis, their participation could always be laundered to hide their contributions."[55]

The silent majority existed in that there were voters who went out and delivered the White House to Donald Trump. However, the organization, operation, building and expansion of that majority to the size that it impacted the election was directly funded, supported, and, in many ways, created by the Mercers and their acolytes. All this attention was an unwelcome position for Robert Mercer, to put it lightly. This led to his decision at the end of 2018 to cut all political spending, according to Bloomberg.[56] The writing on the wall began with a marked decrease to $2.9 million in spending for the 2018 elections. That was a third of what they spent for the 2016 presidential election as well as the preceding 2014 midterms. Between the dissolution of Cambridge Analytica, a falling out with Bannon, protests outside his home in Long Island, and efforts to push university endowments to move their funds away from Renaissance, it seems a grassroots movement may have been sufficient push-back to reduce the influence of the Mercers' astroturf.

CHAPTER 9
PIPELINES OF ASTROTURF

The Keystone Pipeline is an oil pipeline system that runs through North America carrying synthetic crude oil and diluted bitumen from the oil sands, a mixture of sand and oil used for transporting the latter, of Canada. First commissioned in 2010, it is wholly owned by the TransCanada Corporation. In Canada, it originates in Alberta's Western Canadian Sedimentary Basin and in the United States it cuts through Montana, North and South Dakota, Nebraska, Kansas, and Missouri en route to destinations in Illinois, Texas, and Oklahoma.

The pipeline is divided into four phases. The original Keystone Pipeline delivers oil from Hardisty, Alberta, to a junction at Steele City, Nebraska, continuing to Wood River Refinery in Roxana, Illinois, and Patoka Oil Terminal Hub near Patoka, Illinois. It was completed in June 2010 and totaled 2,147 miles. The second phase, completed in February 2011 and dubbed the Keystone-Cushing extension, ran 291 miles from Steele City to Cushing, Oklahoma. The Gulf Coast Extension, the third phase, which totaled 487 miles from Cushing to Port Arthur, Texas, and ran parallel to Houston, Texas, was completed in January 2014.

Politics were injected into the discussion surrounding the project with phase four, nicknamed Keystone XL for its substantial extension of the project. The discussion surrounded a lateral pipeline planned from the main terminal in Hardisty to Baker, Montana, in order for light crude oil from the

Williston Basin to be added before finally continuing on to the central location in Steele City.

In 2015, President Barack Obama rejected the fourth phase after six years of review dating back to the original proposal and prior to any pipes being completed. That political move was the impetus for a proxy battle between climate change advocates and the supporters of fossil fuels.

At the time of the argument over the fourth phase, the amount completed was already a game changer within the US oil industry. The initial two phases had a delivery capacity of 590,000 barrels daily headed to refineries in the Midwest, with phase three more than doubling the load with a 700,000 barrel per day capacity headed to Texas. This represented a significant portion of the 9.4 million average barrels per day in US oil production.

Back in 2011, when two of the four phases of Keystone had been completed, members of the oil industry looked to combat the growing tide of anti-pipeline sentiment and energy.

As the State Department debated the fate of the proposal, those on both sides of the argument took to the streets to fight for their voices to be heard and to Twitter, which has become the breeding ground for many grassroots movements. Among the topics trending on the subject was "#tarsands." Among the tweets was a notable common refrain "#tarsands the truth is out." The slew of tweets with that wording were followed by a link to the American Petroleum Institute's (API) webpage about the tar sands.

The site as it stood at the time (it has since been taken down) featured posts highlighting the positive aspects of oil sands. Posts included arguments on numerous fronts, including:

Economic: "The Canadian Energy Research Institute (CERI) has completed a study of the impact of developing Alberta's oil sands . . . The report shows that in 2010 80,000 U.S. jobs were supported by existing oil sands projects but that without additional pipeline capacity, substantial future benefits will be lost. In particular, Keystone XL pipeline alone could support close to 85,000 U.S. jobs in 2020. Without any pipeline constraints, oil sands development could support 600,000 U.S. jobs by 2035."[1]

Political: "The administration's decision to ban oil and natural gas development in the Atlantic, Pacific and the eastern Gulf of Mexico for the next seven years exacerbates an ongoing problem for the United States: Despite calls for energy independence, the nation could become more reliant on oil from other countries. Fortunately, one of the world's foremost oil producing countries is right next door. In recent years, Canada has become the largest supplier of oil to the United States. An estimated 2 million barrels of Canadian oil comes over the U.S. border every day, and about half of it is derived from Canada's abundant oil sands."[2]

Scientific: "The oil and natural gas industry remains committed to being a reliable and environmentally-responsible provider of the energy needed to power our economy. Canadian and U.S. companies are making the necessary investments to meet stringent environmental and other regulatory requirements to produce and process oil sands."[3]

Unsurprisingly, the counterarguments to these points were not featured anywhere on the site.

The Rainforest Action Network (RAN), an environmental organization founded in San Francisco, was suspicious of the sudden uptick in Twitter users who read the API website and had interest or knowledge of the finer points of tar sands. RAN charged that the API and other oil lobbies allegiant to them were behind the tweets and that it was fake accounts that had sent them, as chronicled in a *Mother Jones* piece written by Kate Sheppard in August 2011. The "grassroots" support for oil sand production and the Keystone XL pipeline across social media may just have been astroturfing orchestrated by companies slated to turn a huge profit because of the new pipeline and in need of some public support to get it to happen.

The astroturf effort did not conclude with one API link: it was followed by posts from the same accounts that linked to a state-based

API-sponsored group named the Nebraska Energy Forum. That group had also spent lots of time and effort fighting on behalf of tar sand development. Their homepage, as linked in the subsequent tweets, had a similar ring to it as evidenced by an "energy myth" described in a graphic on the bottom of the page:

Myth: The Industry sector is the largest emitter of energy related greenhouse gases. Fact: According to the United States Department of Energy, the residential and commercial sector make up 39% of energy related carbon dioxide emissions, followed by transportation at 34% and industry at 27%.[4]

Going to the Nebraska Energy Forum site more recently automatically redirected to America's Energy Forum, quite the jurisdictional expansion. The site professes that its goal is "bringing experts and verifiable facts to the energy discussion," but a deeper dive illuminates they are "bringing" pro-oil arguments. Their "about us" page, states: "America's Energy Forum is a non-partisan community of concerned citizens committed to two goals: Achieving energy security for our country; Holding our elected officials more accountable in shaping energy policies."[5]

However, it doesn't take a very deep dive to see less than balanced coverage. Consider the tabs on the front page, which offer a diversity of thought including: American Jobs; Local Benefit; Government Revenue; Minority Job Growth; Women in the Industry; Veterans; Opportunity; Seismic Surveys; and Safety. There is not much criticism of oil manufacturing to be found by clicking on any of those options.

This rose-colored-glasses view of emissions is only a piece of the various pro-oil arguments contained on the site. With Keystone opponents citing safety as a key arguement against the pipeline, no irony was lost from a banner in the middle of the site dedicated to the dangerous oil spill at the

Deepwater Horizon offshore drilling site. It read: "America's thoughts and prayers are with all those affected by the oil spill in the Gulf of Mexico. The best minds in industry and government are working to stop the spill, contain the oil and clean up the environment. The accident is unprecedented, and so, too, is the combined response of industry and government."[6]

At the time Sheppard wrote the *Mother Jones* piece, she reached out to API for comment, specifically to see if they were behind any of the accounts and postings, but she did not receive a response. When an employee at RAN, Brant Olson, compiled some of the fake handles, it showed the depth of effort in creating the alleged fake accounts. As Sheppard highlighted in her piece:

Take, for example, droidude7816, just a regular old Star Wars fan from Chicago who's "in a intimate relationship" with his girlfriend Sarah . . . His short self-description also notes, "I own pretty much every starwar movie, action figure etc.," and "I'm also one who cares about the environment." It even has a little photo of some doughy white guy having a light-saber fight with Darth Vader! But then all of his 27 tweets are about the Keystone XL.

There's also SarahMama2, who claims to be just your average mother of a toddler who happens to tweet compulsively about the pipeline. And there's JennyJohnson10, "a single woman that works full time at a fitness center" and has "2 cats 1 dog and 1 snake" but only tweets about the tar sands. Or her Twitter friend kyleland1, who claims to be a Pizza Hut manager from Omaha who believes that "if you like pizza you should also like #keystonexl and the sweet #oilsands it benefits #nebraska."[7]

Sheppard didn't mince words on her opinion of the suspicious twitter accounts, adding "Thanks, oil lobby astroturfers!"[8]

In September 2011, *ThinkProgress* told the story of another front group set up for the pro-Keystone efforts in Nebraska, a key battleground as it was a central point along the proposed path.

The story, by Lee Fang, detailed the efforts taken on by the API in lobbying and astroturfing in the state, but also introduced a new chess piece in oil's fight, the "Partnership to Fuel America" described in a press release as "a major new initiative designed to build a stronger foundation for the U.S.–Canadian energy relationship,"[9] all starting in the battleground state of Nebraska.

According to Fang's reporting, the press release introducing "Partnership to Fuel America" was littered with false statements, including the United States Chamber's Institute for 21st Century Energy exaggerating that it represented three million businesses. Also making a play for local sympathy and said to be rooted in Lincoln, Nebraska, per the press release's dateline, *ThinkProgress* traced their origins back to a Minnesota-based lobbying firm named Public Affairs Company. Digging deeper, they confirmed that a Minneapolis-based Republican consultant, Stacy Thompson, was behind the whole thing.

At the same time these efforts were increasing in complexity and intensity, the backlash against oil pipelines was equally expansive. In August 2011, the Republican governor of Nebraska, Dave Heineman, wrote a letter to administration officials saying, "I am opposed to the proposed route of this pipeline . . . 254 miles of the pipeline would come through Nebraska and be situated directly over the Ogallala Aquifer."[10] Shortly after, Nebraska's pair of senators at the time, Mike Johanns (R) and Ben Nelson (D), made an across the aisle agreement and joined most Democrats in urging Obama to stop the pipeline.

As was the case with other famous astroturfing efforts, a public relations firm played an integral role. As somehow was the case with other astroturfing efforts in this book (Wal-Marting Across America, Americans for Technology Leadership), Edelman Public Relations was involved.

In a blog postdated August 2014, Edelman CEO Richard Edelman, who had publicly apologized for being connected to astroturfing efforts in the past, wrote: "We do not work with astroturf groups and we have never created a website for a client with the intent to deny climate change."[11]

A story published in November 2014 by *Motherboard* highlighted the ways in which Edelman PR went about its astroturfing. This introduced the plan B to Keystone XL's plan A, the Energy East Pipeline.

Environmental advocacy group Greenpeace shared leaked documents from Edelman that showed just how precise and strategic the planning of this astroturf effort was. This pipeline had the same origin, Alberta, a different destination, Quebec, and the same intent, making TransCanada money and spreading tar sands further.

The papers laid out a concerted effort described by *Motherboard* writer Brian Merchant as "part sales pitch, part action plan."[12] It was assembled by the firm's Calgary office and advised TransCanada to fight back against the environmental groups and opposition campaigns by putting together a grassroots campaign advocating the opposite; the problem is, of course, that grassroots campaigns by their very nature cannot be manufactured—they grow naturally.

The aforementioned pipeline being debated north of the border was the Energy East pipeline and was partially a product of Keystone XL delays; it was opposed on many of the same grounds as the XL by activists. As cited by *Motherboard*, the documents talk about working to "[a]dd layers of difficulty for our opponents, distracting them from their mission and causing them to redirect their resources," while creating "supportive third parties, who can in turn put the pressure on, especially when TransCanada can't."[13]

Motherboard also highlighted a document called "Digital Grassroots Advocacy Implementation Plan" from May 2014 that called for a "grassroots mobilization program" beginning with an "action center website."[14] Later that year action.energyeastpipeline.com went live. This served as evidence that the plan laid out in those leaks was enacted to some degree.

Motherboard's request for comment from Edelman went nowhere, but TransCanada told the *New York Times* and Huffington Post that they had "moved forward with implementing certain components of the strategy,"[15] making note that they had foregone the third-party element, the most obvious bit of astroturfing. Greenpeace believed that this was a cop-out, with their research director Mark Floegal telling *Motherboard*, "We have every reason to believe they're doing this."[16]

Motherboard's Brian Merchant laid out just how clear the astroturfing approach was in these documents likely never meant to see the light of day. "The documents quite literally contain a blueprint to build and mobilize a movement—not unlike the Energy Citizens group Edelman helped the American Petroleum Institute assemble to oppose climate legislation in 2009—to publicly rally in favor of the contentious Energy East pipeline,"[17] he wrote. They explicitly laid out their aim to "convert" the average citizen into "advocates" of oil and oil companies.

The documents set a goal of 35,000 advocates, focusing on recruitment and development online through social media, targeted advertising, and setting up websites and email lists. Much like selling subscriptions, the Edelman documents describe a "multiplier platform" built out of Salesforce, a software for keeping track of customers. The unorthodox element was using a platform usually reserved for commercial pursuits for political gain and support for an oil pipeline.

The multiplier software came to Edelman when they acquired Grassroots Enterprise in 2009 and led to advertisements from Edelman about their grassroots outreach capabilities.

As would be expected, a key starting point for the astroturf manual was finding supporters who, based on common logic, could be swayed for big oil, such as union workers set to get pipeline jobs or oil company employees looking to keep their jobs. The next step, as laid out in the documents, was to take a "methodical and deliberate approach designed to convert average citizens into issue activists."[18]

The *Motherboard* story heavily quotes from the leaked documents that tell the story themselves, with use of cleaner language, of how an astroturfing effort is undertaken. To create these grassroots activists, Edelman would look at "how to deepen and broaden each individual's commitment to our cause, using targeted messaging and behavior tracking to directly appeal to the individual's trigger points and develop them from a supporter to an activist to a champion . . . Jointly, these processes create the outputs we need to achieve the outcomes we desire; in short, they provide us a rich base of advocates who passionately understand and support our cause and are willing—more often than not—to do what's asked of them."[19]

When the results don't go swimmingly and potential advocates need more prodding, Edelman stays on top of the issue: "To be clear, not every advocate will do everything we ask of him or her, and not every advocate will have the willingness or ability to become a true champion . . . Accordingly, we must track and monitor how individuals behave and perform so that we can provide them with the materials calls to action that best align with where they are and what they are able to offer—while always pushing them to do just a bit more."[20]

However, to maximize output, even those who were true believers or easy converts would be kept under the watchful eye of the PR firm, "Every grassroots advocate record will be tagged and tracked based on how/where they were recruited, which message stream they responded to and how they perform over time," the report stated. "These metrics will enable us both to tailor outbound communications to user preferences and to enhance future recruitment efforts."[21]

From there, Merchant collected his thoughts and laid out just how telling the documents were: "The world's biggest PR company has, in other words, outlined, in great detail, how it anticipates targeting everyday citizens and convincing them to become pro-oil support troops, and how it intends to collect data on those [who] aren't quite ready to rally to the cause and how to push them over the edge."[22]

Floegal said to *Motherboard* of the leaks, "We've never seen something with quite this level of depth before . . . We've got the whole playbook."[23]

The way the documents discuss this is much like a business discussing costs per acquisition (in this case, of new advocates) and discussing the most effective ways of acquiring the assets (aka recruiting advocates). How this would all play out in practice, according to the leaked documents, would be for Edelman and TransCanada to reach out to a potential recruit on either social media sites, blogs about energy issues, or via email, all while monitoring the responses, engagement, and most effective messaging and platform. At that point, they would be entered into the multiplier to compile data on the recruit. The tactics were not particularly evil, since political campaigns, retail websites, and everything in between use similar approaches. The contrast came from the fact it was an oil company recruiting heralds to deliver a message that aided their bottom line significantly.

As Merchant put it, "these documents underline how sophisticated corporate efforts to 'mobilize grassroots advocates'—to grow their own astroturf—have become."[24]

Around a similar time, the *New York Times* had the same documents and was told by a TransCanada spokesman that they, "confirmed that the company had followed Edelman's advice to create a network of allies."[25]

Unsurprisingly, the Canadian strategy was also retrofitted for use in the United States: "Companies like ExxonMobil, Chevron, Shell, and Haliburton (and many more) have all made key investments in building permanent advocacy assets and programs to support their lobbying, outreach, and policy efforts. In launching a program like this, TransCanada will be in good company with a strong roadmap to follow."[26]

The extent of Edelman's connections to oil and where exactly those efforts had been deployed is unclear. Nonetheless, the names they dropped raise an air of speculation that can spread far and wide. Edelman does not make all of its clients public. We do know that the 2009 acquisition of Grassroots Enterprises gave them the ability to have these capabilities, and that there is well-documented work over several years and multiple millions of dollars with API.

As Merchant concluded, "by simultaneously denying involvement with any astroturf groups at all and running what amounts to an in-house digital astroturf generator, Edelman is pioneering a murky future for public relations indeed."[27]

When Greenpeace obtained the documents, a story was posted by Jesse Coleman on their website in November 2014.

"Sophisticated PR plans like the one created by Edelman have become vital to fossil fuel companies, who have seen their traditionally strong sway over politicians weaken in response to massive pressure from voters concerned about climate change. As seen by the failed Keystone XL vote Tuesday night, the fossil fuel industry has been forced into waging what Edelman refers to as 'perpetual campaigns' against concerned communities in order to build environmentally dangerous projects," wrote Coleman. "The Edelman plan carries several hallmarks of astroturf campaigns, including the promise of creating grassroots support."[28]

As is key to correctly astroturfed agendas, Coleman also remarked that they aimed to make the swell of support look natural: "All told, Edelman hoped to use all of TransCanada workers as part of the astroturf campaign. Edelman plans on using the astroturf plan to influence media, the public, politicians, and regulatory agencies."

Greenpeace also discovered the unsavory history of Edelman, which appeared in several chapters of this book:

Edelman has a long history of working on astroturf campaigns. In 1978, Edelman offered the tobacco industry a "total program" to avoid smoking bans, which included industry funded, seemingly independent smoking groups to defend the tobacco industry. More recently Edelman has worked for the American Legislative Exchange Council (ALEC), a stealth lobbying organization that denies climate change science and opposes renewable energy. Edelman also works for The American Petroleum Institute, Exxon, Shell, Chevron, and other oil companies on an astroturf effort called Energy Citizens.[29]

The same leaked documents were also reviewed and assessed by *PR Watch*, which found that, despite the planned pipeline starting, ending, and running through Canadian soil, the campaign was set to run out of Washington, DC. In excerpts published by Ian Austen in the *New York Times*, the planning documents of the Energy East pipeline aimed to expand the range of where the tar sands could be sent in order to send it south with the Keystone path to the Gulf of Mexico being uncertain.

The *Times* story revealed plans more insidious than just converting potential supporters, including campaigns pressuring activists in order to stymie their efforts. They looked to do opposition research on activist groups, including the Council of Canadians, Ecology Ottawa, the David Suzuki Foundation, and Equiterre.[30]

Austen led the story with a blunt description of the leaks, saying, "The advice from a top American public relations firm was simple: A Canadian pipeline company should take aim at its opposition." He quoted from their leaks, saying "a perpetual campaign to protect and enhance the value of the Energy East Pipeline and to help inoculate TransCanada from potential attacks in any arena."[31]

TransCanada tried to stay above the controversy in the pages of the *Times* with spokesman James Millar saying that the documents were more a proposal from Edelman and less a plan that was enacted. Nonetheless, he admitted they investigated opponents and created a network of support but did not weaponize third parties against opponents.[32]

The *Times* story included what some of the opponents of Energy East and Keystone thought of these revelations, including Maude Barlow, national chairwoman of the Council of Canadians, who was quoted as saying, "I'm a grandmother . . . To me it's a sign of desperation . . . It's basically all wrong, and it takes away from the public debate we should be having."[33] Likewise, Ben Powless from Ecology Ottawa was surprised that his nine person team would be targeted by the powerhouse that is Edelman, adding, "To me, it's a smear campaign really trying to shut down the voices of local people who have legitimate concerns."[34]

Millar claimed TransCanada hired Edelman for help with speaking French[35] as they have a presence in the francophone province of Quebec.

PR Watch quoted the Edelman documents, saying that they would like to set up "layers of difficulty for opponents, [and they would] work with third parties and arm them with the information they need to pressure opponents and distract them from their mission. . . . Third-party voices must be identified, recruited and heard to build an echo chamber of aligned voices."[36]

PR Watch went on to detail efforts to have third parties do their dirty work, including recruiting professors to speak on behalf of the pipelines (of course, with a preference that they not disclose the fact they had been recruited).

That interest in experts extended to who was brought into the operation, namely Michael Krempasky, who has connections to the Koch brothers' "Americans for Prosperity" and is the cofounder of RedState.org, a conservative blog. Krempasky had connections to two astroturfing efforts in the Tea Party, as well as "Working Families for Walmart." Krempasky first became involved with the Kochs at their Leadership Institute, which had such illustrious alumni as James O'Keefe, a conservative political activist with no shortage of controversy.

The organization successfully recruited other GOP operatives, along with Krempasky, including both GOP spokesperson Nate Bailey and former John McCain campaign staffer Brian McNeill. The leaked documents showed some of the data that Edelman was leaning on and exploring for their efforts, including, as cited in *PR Watch* by Lisa Graves, 16 percent of Canadians had a favorable view of tar sands and 36 percent held a favorable view of methane gas.[37] Edelman also asked whether they could change the perception that oil sands are worse than natural gas. Additionally, more than a third of Québécois (i.e., the people of Quebec) believe in higher toxicity and corrosiveness in oil extracted from sands.[38] There was a marked increase in the amount of people worried the pipeline could be tampered with, partially owing to a previous accident with a train carrying oil in Quebec that killed forty-seven Canadians.[39]

President Obama was not only about to shut down Keystone but was also critical of Energy East at the time, bemoaning that it "would be providing the ability of Canada to pump their oil, send it through our land, down to the Gulf, where it will be sold everywhere else."[40]

Despite all the oil spill potential and tax subsidies and related issues being north of Obama's territory in the plan, his progressive stance on the threat posed by climate change was a source for his opposition to Energy East and Keystone alike. Estimates quoted in *PR Watch* put the damage at thirty million tons of greenhouse emissions annually without mentioning potential damage to wildlife and water.[41]

As James Hansen wrote in an op-ed in the *New York Times*, the completion of the pipeline "will be game over for the planet."[42] That stark threat was trumped by dollars and cents, as mentioned in *PR Watch*:

"According to a report by Lee Fang for The Investigative Fund, Edelman was paid more than $50 million to run the PR campaign of the American Petroleum Institute (API), to push politicians to approve the Keystone XL pipeline, support tax deduction for the oil industry companies that fund API, and press for expanded drilling in America's national parks."[43]

When discussing the Energy East effort, the Huffington Post said of the pipeline that it "has been described as an 'oil route around Obama' amid political wrangling over Keystone XL in the United States."[44]

They used the same Greenpeace leak for source material and said that the documents "show a company increasingly concerned about the fate of Keystone XL, which would connect the tar sands with Gulf Coast refineries," additionally observing that, "TransCanada's Energy East also faces increasing opposition, as does a proposed pipeline to the west, Enbridge's Northern Gateway."[45]

In the Huffington Post story by Kate Sheppard, Keith Stewart of Greenpeace Canada said, "TransCanada has been saying, 'If you don't let us build Keystone, we will build to the east . . . These documents show that they're clearly worried about the Energy East pipeline as well. It's going to face just as rough a ride as Keystone or Northern Gateway."[46]

Sheppard's story cited an organization document from the campaign that lays out a "Promote, Respond, Pressure approach" to "respond to allegations and protect the company."[47] She quoted a passage from the leaks:

Add layers of difficulty for our opponents, distracting them from their mission and causing them to redirect their resources. We cannot allow our opponents to have a free pass. They will use any piece of information they can find to attack TransCanada and this project—attacks are part of a larger, modern oppositional effort to silence those on the other side . . . This point should particularly be made in communication to supportive third parties, who can in turn put the pressure on, especially when TransCanada can't.[48]

When Sheppard approached TransCanada, she got a corporate response with their spokesman saying, "We have been working with Edelman for several months now and appreciate the support they have provided in helping us better engage in the public conversation, both in Quebec and the rest of Canada. Edelman was chosen because of their presence in Quebec and their ability to understand the culture. This is an important component for

TransCanada's communications outreach as we move forward with this project."[49]

"If astroturf is using artificial grassroots to support a corporate agenda, this is clearly it," said Kert Davies, executive director of the Climate Investigations Center, which has been investigating the role of public relations firms in energy and climate campaigns. "This is a small window into the type of campaigns that oil companies and the American Petroleum Institute have been running for many years to try to affect the political arena."[50]

Those who wanted to see tar sands more easily moved and the profits that would come as a result diversified their efforts to make it happen.

Consider the site opechatesgays.com. The site and its social media component serve to further advertise the idea that those represented in the Organization of the Petroleum Exporting Countries (or OPEC) have abysmal records on treatment of homosexuals. It also juxtaposed the stellar record of Canada with the same group. For some reason, this logic was presented as reason to build the Keystone pipeline and import[51] tar sand to the United States from Canada.

Queers for Climate, with a far more real membership than their opposition, dates back to at least the 2014 People's Climate March. They have opposing views to the aforementioned website as evidenced by their nomenclature, pointing out that politically[52] those who are for LGBT rights are typically environmentally friendly. However, the proposition that one's stance on oil use and the climate has anything to do with stances on LGBT rights is a bit of stretch on both sides.

This effort is something known as pinkwashing, which uses LGBT issues as propaganda for unrelated political gain. Tweets with a similar intent were highlighted in a piece from the *Daily Beast* by Jay Michaelson. One cited tweet read, "Say yes to Keystone XL and no to homophobic OPEC oil!"[53]

Along with pinkwashing, it is also astroturfing. Opechatesgays.com is a part of a larger organization known as Ethical Oil. That umbrella group does not divulge where it's funding comes from but, according to

Michaelson, "is linked to a network of Conservative party leaders, petrodollars, and right-wing media outlets."[54]

The ideas trumpeted by Ethical Oil began with a 2010 book by Ezra Levant titled *Ethical Oil: The Case for Canada's Oil Sands*, as reported by a climate blog called *desmogblog*.[55] From there, the Canadian right-wing Sun Media Corporation (which folded in 2010), then-Prime Minister Stephen Harper, and conservative online bloggers spread the ideas.

The rest of the campaign is the astroturf playbook. As the *Daily Beast* read: "Americans are familiar with these kinds of shenanigans—the right wing 'talking points' circulated between Republican leaders, Fox News, CTTs (Conservative Think Tanks) in Washington, and above all, Grover Norquist, who has held his Wednesday morning messaging-coordination meetings for two decades now—although he is now being eclipsed by an even farther-right network called Groundswell."[56]

Desmogblog went further into the source of the astroturf efforts. Hamish and Kathryn Marshall founded Ethical Oil and the subsidiary opechatesgays.com. Hamish had experience in that type of work with his Go New-Clear Productions, a communications firm featuring more than fifty websites with connections to, according to analyses of the webpages form the piece, "over 50 websites connected primarily to the Conservative Party of Canada, the Wildrose Alliance Party, EthicalOil.org, and other right-wing causes and politicians."[57]

They also had sophisticated clients in Finance Minister Joe Oliver, and Minister of Employment and Social Development and Minister for Multiculturalism Jason Kenney. Hamish had been a former staffer of the prime minister. A prominent conservative blogger named Alykhan Velshi had left Ethical Oil to work for Prime Minister Harper as director of planning and before Ethical Oil worked for Kenney. The connections continued, with Levant serving as one of two directors on the board of Ethical Oil along with the tar sands developer's lawyer Thomas Ross.

As is the case with astroturfing, Michaelson pointed out, "None of this is illegal; it's just a revolving door between the Conservative government, the oil industry, and a fake nonprofit."[58]

The banner on opechatesgays.com is provocative, asking visitors to "Please donate now to promote this grassroots ad online."[59] Upon investigation, it doesn't hold up much as grassroots. There is more, with "fight back against oil tyrants" and "President Obama, I support pipelines from Canada. Let's buy Ethical Oil and stop propping up OPEC regimes of hatred" also on the site. They also used to document instances of anti-gay incidents in Nigeria, Saudi Arabia, and Iran. Where exactly the donations they begged for go is anyone's guess.

"Ethical Oil refuses to disclose its donors, and Kathryn Marshall deftly declined to answer whether it has taken money from the petroleum industry, or, in particular, foreign companies that own Canadian and U.S. firms," wrote Michaelson. "Opechatesgays is where . . . pinkwashing meet Astroturf."[60]

President Donald Trump overrode President Obama's decision, and took actions to allow for the completion of the pipeline. Coming just four days after the inauguration and fourteen months after his predecessor disallowed the fourth phase, Trump signed presidential memoranda reviving not only the Keystone XL, but also the Dakota Access Pipeline, keeping a specific campaign promise through executive order and adding to his pro-coal reputation. It seems the astroturfing was for naught, being superseded by two separate administrations. As of now, the Keystone pipeline is in the works with some push back from the courts causing hiccups. The Dakota Access Pipeline, on the other hand, is fully operational.

CONCLUSION

I n these turbulent times, two of the great threats to our democracy are money in politics and the weakening of the power of the truth. Those two threats are both present when astroturfing is deployed. At its very essence, a democratic system is reliant on the will of the people being the catalyzing force for the direction of the republic, so when there is a price tag on creating a "will of the people," that foundational requirement is eroded.

One would be hard pressed to find a better time to visit this perilous reality. The Trump administration contains a laundry list of lobbyists and industry executives given the power to regulate and oversee the very agencies they once answered to in the private sector. Our current politics also see a reduction in how unanimous the idea of the truth is. Many Americans are more than happy to accept whatever truth fits into their preconceived notions and agendas in lieu of searching for a singular fact-based idea.

The public sector faces similarly precarious conditions as more mergers and acquisitions increase the size of major companies and reduce the amount of competition in sectors important to everyday life such as healthcare or finance. If these companies can avoid answering for their practices or even cultivate support through an astroturf campaign, they will be able to run amok.

The power of the people is enshrined in the First Amendment and electoral process more so than any other part of the American experiment. When speech can be simulated, press can be tricked, assembly can be purchased, and petitions can be forged, what power is left? When campaigns can be fueled so inextricably by special interests and the ruling class, who is really choosing the people's representation? These are the difficult questions that may just decide the future of the country.

In writing this book, one thing was made abundantly clear, the *Citizens United* Supreme Court decision is among the most dangerous changes in politics in recent memory. As long as that remains the prevailing law of the land, money will be as important, if not more so, than winning over the people when it comes to deciding our representation.

Both sides of the aisle agree on very little. At least in rhetoric, they both decry money in politics. If that refrain is true, and not just talk, something should be done imminently to reduce the ability for private money to have such an outsize impact on political maneuvering. In these times, democracy depends on it.

NOTES

INTRODUCTION

1. Shaban, Hamza, "Two senators say their identities were stolen in fake net neutrality comments to the FCC." *Washington Post*, May 23, 2018. https://www.washingtonpost.com/news/the-switch/wp/2018/05/23/two -senators-say-their-identities-were-stolen-in-fake-net-neutrality-comments -to-the-fcc/?noredirect=on&utm_term=.aa7319edd916.

CHAPTER 1

2. James V. Grimaldi and Paul Overberg, "Millions of People Post Comments on Federal Regulations. Many Are Fake.," *The Wall Street Journal*, December 12, 2017, https://www.wsj.com/articles/millions-of-people -post-comments-on-federal-regulations-many-are-fake-1513099188.
3. Ibid.
4. Ibid.
5. Ibid.
6. Ibid.
7. Ibid.
8. Ibid.
9. Ibid.
10. Ibid.

11. Ibid.

12. Ibid.

13. George Monbiot, "These astroturf libertarians are the real threat to internet democracy," *The Guardian,* December 13, 2010, https://www .theguardian.com/commentisfree/libertycentral/2010/dec/13/astroturf -libertarians-internet-democracy.

14. Ibid.

15. Ibid.

16. Ibid.

17. Ibid.

18. George Monbiot, "The need to protect the internet from 'astroturfing' grows ever more urgent," *The Guardian*, February 23, 2011, https:// www.theguardian.com/environment/georgemonbiot/2011/feb/23/need -to-protect-internet-from-astroturfing.

19. Happy Rockefeller, UPDATED: The HB Gary Email That Should Concern Us All," *Daily Kos,* February 16, 2011, https://www.dailykos .com/stories/2011/02/16/945768/-UPDATED:-The-HB-Gary-Email -That-Should-Concern-Us-All.

20. Ibid.

21. Adam Bienkov, "Astroturfing: what is it and why does it matter?" *The Guardian*, February 8, 2012, https://www.theguardian.com /commentisfree/2012/feb/08/what-is-astroturfing.

22. Ibid.

CHAPTER 2

1. George Monbiot, "The Tea Party movement: deluded and inspired by billionaires," *The Guardian*, October 25, 2010, https://www.theguardian .com/commentisfree/cifamerica/2010/oct/25/tea-party-koch-brothers.

2. "About," The John Birch Society, accessed 2017, https://www.jbs.org /about-jbs.

3. Jane Mayer, "Covert Operations," The New Yorker, August 30, 2010, https://www.newyorker.com/magazine/2010/08/30/covert-operations.

4. Ibid.

5. Ibid.

6. Ibid.

7. "About Mercatus," Mercatus Center, accessed 2017, https://www.mercatus.org/about.

8. Bob Davis, "In Washington, Tiny Think Tank Wields Big Stick on Regulation," The Wall Street Journal, July 16, 2014, https://www.wsj.com/articles/SB10899439655506646.

9. Ibid.

10. Ibid.

11. http://vault.sierraclub.org/sierra/200207/thinktank_printable.asp.

12. Mayer, "Covert."

13. Ibid.

14. Andrew Goldman, "The Billionaire's Party," New York Magazine, July 25, 2010, http://nymag.com/nymag/features/67285/.

15. Tim Mak, "The Left's Billion Dollar Tea Party Lie," FrumForum, May 10, 2010, http://frumforum.com/entry/the-lefts-billion-dollar-tea-party-lie.

16. Ibid.

17. (Astro) Turf Wars, Taki Oldham, 2010, https://www.imdb.com/title/tt1899098/.

18. Barack Obama, Austin, Texas, August, 9, 2010, https://obamawhitehouse.archives.gov/the-press-office/2010/08/09/remarks-president-a-dnc-finance-event-austin-texas.

19. Ibid.

20. Mark Ames and Mike Elk, Big Brothers: Thought Control at Koch, The Nation, April 20, 2011, https://www.thenation.com/article/big-brothers-thought-control-koch/.

21. Ibid.

22. Daniel Shulman, *Sons of Wichita: How the Koch Brothers Became America's Most Powerful and Private Dynasty* (New York: Grand Central Publishing, 2015).

23. Kris Hundley, "Billionaire's role in hiring decisions at Florida State University raises questions," *Tampa Bay Times*, May 9, 2011, http://www.tampabay.com/news/business/billionaires-role-in-hiring-decisions-at-florida-state-university-raises/1168680.

24. Monbiot, "Deluded."

25. Mayer, "Covert."

26. Kate Zernike, "Tea Party Set to Win Enough Races for Wide Influence," *The New York Times*, October 14, 2010. https://www.nytimes.com/2010/10/15/us/politics/15teaparty.html?mtrref=archive.nytimes.com.

27. "Just 32% of Tea Party candidates win," *NBC News*, November 3, 2010, http://firstread.nbcnews.com/_news/2010/11/03/5403120-just-32-of-tea-party-candidates-win.

28. Mayer, "Covert."

29. Kenneth Vogel, "The Kochs fight back," *Politico*, February 2, 2011, https://www.politico.com/story/2011/02/the-kochs-fight-back-048624.

30. Mayer, "Covert."

31. Ibid.

32. Ben Smith, "The Koch money," *Politico*, August 23, 2010, https://www.politico.com/blogs/ben-smith/2010/08/the-koch-money-028750.

33. Mayer, "Covert."

CHAPTER 3

1. "THE 2000 CAMPAIGN; Excerpts from McCain's Speech," *The New York Times*, February 20, 2000, https://www.nytimes.com/2000/02/20/us/the-2000-campaign-excerpts-from-mccain-s-speech.html.

2. Beth Reinhard, "Bush strategist shares insight on '00 recount," *The Miami Herald*, May 17, 2008.

3. Benjamin Sarlin, "A GOP Dirty Trickster Has Second Thoughts," *The Daily Beast*, November 20, 2008, https://www.thedailybeast.com/a-gop -dirty-trickster-has-second-thoughts.

4. Ibid.

5. Reinhard, "Bush strategist."

6. John Lantigua, "Miami's rent-a-riot," *Salon*, November 28, 2000, https://www.salon.com/2000/11/28/miami_8/.

7. Joe Conason, "Right-Wingers Praise Antics of Bush Thugs," *The New York Observer*, December 3, 2000.

8. Ibid.

9. Dana Canedy and Dexter Filkins, "COUNTING THE VOTE: MIAMI-DADE COUNTY; A Wild Day in Miami, With an End to Recounting, and Democrats' Going to Court," *The New York Times*, November 23, 2000, https://www.nytimes.com/2000/11/23/us/counting-vote-miami-dade -county-wild-day-miami-with-end-recounting-democrats.html.

10. Ibid.

11. Ibid.

12. Tim Padgett, "Mob Scene in Miami," *Time Magazine*, November 26, 2000, http://content.time.com/time/nation/article/0,8599,89450,00 .html.

13. Reinhard, "Bush strategist."

14. "Sweeney and the Siege of Miami," *Salon,* November 28, 2000, https:// slate.com/news-and-politics/2000/11/sweeney-and-the-siege-of-miami .html.

15. Dennis Cauchon and Jim Drinkard, "Florida voter errors cost Gore the election," *USA Today*, May 11, 2001, https://usatoday30.usatoday.com /news/washington/2001-05-10-recountmain.html.

16. Ibid.

17. "The Long Count," White House 2000: Post-Election Polls, PollingReport
.com December 14–21, 2000, https://www.chicagomanualofstyle.org
/tools_citationguide/citation-guide-1.html.

18. Henry Pulizzi, "White House Brushes Off Health-Care Protests," *The
Wall Street Journal*, August 4, 2009, https://www.wsj.com/articles
/SB124939676158504833.

CHAPTER 4

1. "US productivity growth, 1995–2000," *McKinsey Global Institute*,
October, 2001, https://www.mckinsey.com/featured-insights/americas
/us-productivity-growth-1995-2000.

2. "Wal-Mart trade deficit with China cost more than 400,000 jobs from
2001 to 2013," *Economic Policy Institute*, December 9, 2015, https://
www.epi.org/press/walmart-trade-deficit-with-china-cost-more-than
-400000-jobs-from-2001-to-2013/.

3. Emek Basker, "Job Creation or Destruction? Labor Market Effects of
Wal-Mart Expansion," *University of Missouri,* 2002, https://www
.mitpressjournals.org/doi/pdf/10.1162/0034653053327568.

4. Stephan J. Goetz and Hema Swaminathan, "Wal-Mart and County-
Wide Poverty," *Pennsylvania State University*, October 18, 2004,
https://aese.psu.edu/research/centers/cecd/research/wal-mart-and-county
-wide-poverty/full-study.

5. Dr. Raj Patel, Melbourne, Australia, April 5, 2009, https://www.abc
.net.au/radionational/programs/bigideas/food-glorious-food/3132832.

6. Sebastian Mallaby, "Progressive Wal-Mart. Really," *The Washington
Post*, November 28, 2005, http://www.washingtonpost.com/wp-dyn
/content/article/2005/11/27/AR2005112700687.html.

7. George Will, "Democrats Vs. Wal-Mart," *The Washington Post*, September 14, 2006, http://www.washingtonpost.com/wp-dyn/content/article
/2006/09/13/AR2006091301573.html.

8. Pallavi Gogoi, "Wal-Mart's Jim and Laura: The Real Story," *Bloomberg Businessweek*, October 10, 2006, https://www.bloomberg.com/news /articles/2006-10-09/wal-marts-jim-and-laura-the-real-storybusinessweek -business-news-stock-market-and-financial-advice.

9. Ibid.

10. Ibid.

11. Ibid.

12. Ibid.

13. Ibid.

14. Ibid.

15. Laura, "The Final Word," *Wal-Marting Across America (Archive)*, October 12, 2006, https://web.archive.org/web/20061111041158/http:// walmartingacrossamerica.com/.

16. Jonathan Rees, "An Open Letter to 'Jim' and 'Laura'," *The Writing on the Wal*, October 3, 2006, http://thewritingonthewal.net/?p=1387.

17. Ibid.

18. Jonathan Rees, "Another Open Letter to 'Jim' and 'Laura'," *The Writing on the Wal*, October 3, 2006, http://thewritingonthewal.net/?p=1391.

19. Gogoi, "Real Story."

20. Howard Kurtz, "Post Photographer Repays Group for Trip Expenses," *The Washington Post*, October 12, 2006, http://www.washingtonpost .com/wp-dyn/content/article/2006/10/11/AR2006101101658.html.

21. Ibid.

22. Ibid.

23. Ibid.

24. Gogoi, "Real Story."

25. Kurtz, "Post Photographer."

26. Mark Glaser, "What do you think about the fake Wal-Mart blogs by Edelman PR?," *MediaShift*, October 20, 2006, http://mediashift.org/2006/10 /what-do-you-think-about-the-fake-wal-mart-blogs-by-edelman-pr293/.

27. "PR firm admits it's behind Wal-Mart blogs," *CNN Money*, October 20, 2006, https://money.cnn.com/2006/10/20/news/companies /walmart_blogs/.

28. Edelman Apologizes For Fake Walmart Blog," *Consumerist*, October 17, 2006, https://consumerist.com/2006/10/17/edelman-apologizes-for -fake-walmart-blog/.

29. Consumerist, "Edelman Apologizes."

30. "New Word For Corporate Shill Blogs," *Consumerist*, October 19, 2006, https://consumerist.com/2006/10/19/new-word-for-corporate -shill-blogs/.

31. Gogoi, "Real Story."

32. Jack Schofield, "What's a flog—a fake blog?" *The Guardian*, October 16, 2006, https://www.theguardian.com/technology/blog/2006/oct/16 /whatsafloga.

33. Kiley Skene, "A PR Case Study: Wal-Marting Across America," *News Generation*, April 4, 2014, https://www.newsgeneration.com/2014/04 /04/pr-case-study-walmarting-across-america/.

34. Gogoi, "Real Story."

35. Pallavi Gogoi, "Wal-Mart vs. the Blogosphere," *Bloomberg Business-week*, October 17, 2006, https://www.bloomberg.com/news/articles /2006-10-17/wal-mart-vs-dot-the-blogospherebusinessweek-business -news-stock-market-and-financial-advice.

36. Ibid.

37. Ibid.

38. Mya Frazier, "Edelman Eats Humble Pie," *AdAge*, October 19, 2006, https://adage.com/article/news/edelman-eats-humble-pie/112588/.

39. Ibid.

CHAPTER 5

1. https://oag.ca.gov/news/press-releases/statement-microsoft-antitrust -lawsuit-california-attorney-general-bill-lockyer.

2. Ibid.

3. John R. Wilke, "Microsoft Drafts Settlement Proposal, Hoping to Resolve Antitrust Lawsuit," *The Wall Street Journal*, September 10, 2008, https://www.wsj.com/articles/SB1000076767888491506.

4. Ibid.

5. Ibid.

6. Ibid.

7. "Microsoft's Teflon Bill," *Bloomberg*, November 30, 1998, https://www .bloomberg.com/news/articles/1998-11-29/microsofts-teflon-bill.

8. Ibid.

9. Ibid.

10. Ibid.

11. "Who's Behind the Pro-Microsoft Poll?" *Slate*, March 27, 2000, https:// slate.com/business/2000/03/who-s-behind-the-pro-microsoft-poll.html.

12. "Poll shows most oppose Microsoft breakup," *CNET*, January 2, 2000, https://www.cnet.com/news/poll-shows-most-oppose-microsoft -breakup/.

13. Ibid.

14. Ibid.

15. Joseph Menn and Edmund Sanders, "Lobbyists Tied to Microsoft Wrote Citizens' Letters," *Los Angeles Times*, August 23, 2001, http:// articles.latimes.com/2001/aug/23/news/mn-37472.

16. Ibid.

17. Ibid.

18. Ibid.

19. Ibid.

20. Simon English, "Back from the grave to boost Microsoft case," *The Telegraph*, August 24, 2001, https://www.telegraph.co.uk/finance /2731227/Back-from-the-grave-to-boost-Microsoft-case.html.

21. Robyn Weisman, "Report: Phony 'Grassroots' Campaign Orchestrated by Microsoft," *News Factor*, August 23, 2001, http://www.newsfactor .com/perl/story/13046.html.

22. Ibid.

23. "About This Site," TechRights, accessed 2017, http://techrights.org /about-the-site/.

24. John Broder, "Microsoft Tries Another Court: Public Opinion," *The New York Times*, June 12, 2000, https://www.nytimes.com/2000/06/12 /business/microsoft-tries-another-court-public-opinion.html.

25. Dr. Roy Schestowitz, Another Microsoft Shill: Americans for Technology Leadership (ATL), *TechRights*, September 1, 2008, http://techrights .org/2008/09/01/americans-for-technology-leadership-atl/.

26. Joshua Marshall, "Mr. Gates Goes to Washington," *The American Prospect*, December 19, 2001, http://prospect.org/article/mr-gates-goes -washington.

27. Robert X. Cringley "The Once and Future King: Now the Only Way Microsoft Can Die is by Suicide," *The Pulpit*. April 8, 2004, https:// www.webcitation.org/query?id=1298667420478042.

28. Ibid.

29. Ibid.

30. Ibid.

31. Ibid.

32. https://www.sec.gov/Archives/edgar/data/789019/000119312508162768 /d10k.htm#tx31450_3.

CHAPTER 6

1. "National Smokers Alliance," *Source Watch*, accessed 2017, https://www.sourcewatch.org/index.php/National_Smokers_Alliance.

2. John C. Stauber, "Smokers' Hacks: the Tobacco Lobby's PR Front Groups," PR Watch, volume 1, number 1, Third Quarter 1994.

3. Ibid.

4. Ibid.

5. Ibid.

6. Ibid.

7. Peter Stone, National Journal, May 28, 1994.

8. PR Watch, "Smokers."

9. Ibid.

10. Ibid.

11. Ibid.

12. Ibid.

13. Don Lee, "Tobacco Group Campaigns to Head Off Bar Smoking Ban," *Los Angeles Times*, February 21, 1996, http://articles.latimes.com/1996-02-21/business/fi-38269_1_bar-smoking-tobacco.

14. Tom Shales, "SHRIEK! CHIC! IT'S MORTON DOWNEY!," *The Washington Post*, July 6, 1988, https://www.washingtonpost.com/archive/lifestyle/1988/07/06/shriek-chic-its-morton-downey/a6e7fdd7-611d-417b-816e-df33390e156a/?utm_term=.96071ac57994.

15. Ibid.

16. Ibid.

17. Ibid.

18. Ibid.

19. Ibid.

20. "'Mort the Mouth' Downey Jr. Dies," *The Washington Post*, March 14, 2001, https://www.washingtonpost.com/archive/local/2001/03/14/mort

-the-mouth-downey-jr-die/30c00e45-41ad-44c3-b51c-b2fa190f841f/?utm
_term=.8220b46b0ca8.

21. Shales, "SHRIEK!."

22. Associated Press "Trash TV icon Morton Downey Jr. dies," *CNN*,
March 13, 2001, http://archive.li/LF9le#selection-1161.0-1156.5.

23. Ibid.

24. Ibid.

25. Ibid.

26. Wolfgang Saxon, "Morton Downey Jr., 67, Combative TV Host," *The
New York Times*, March 14, 2001, https://www.nytimes.com/2001
/03/14/arts/morton-downey-jr-67-combative-tv-host.html.

27. *The Washington Post*, "Mort the Mouth."

28. http://transcripts.cnn.com/TRANSCRIPTS/0103/13/lkl.00.html.

29. Myron Levin, "Cancer Diagnosis Prompts Downey to Switch Sides,"
Los Angeles Times, July 12, 1996, http://articles.latimes.com/1996-07
-12/business/fi-23291_1_lung-cancer.

30. Ibid.

31. Ibid.

32. Ibid.

33. Ibid.

34. Ibid.

35. Ibid.

36. https://profiles.nlm.nih.gov/ps/retrieve/Narrative/NN/p-nid/60.

37. Glenn Frankel, "Decades After Declaration, War on Smoking Begins,"
The Washington Post, August 24, 1996, http://www.washingtonpost.com
/wp-srv/national/longterm/tobacco/stories/war.htm.

38. Ibid.

39. Ibid.

40. Ibid.

41. Tom Kuntz, "The National Smokers Alliance; Got a Light? How About The Flame of Freedom?," *The New York Times,* September 21, 1997, https://www.nytimes.com/1997/09/21/weekinreview/word-for-word-national-smokers-alliance-got-light-about-flame-freedom.html.

42. Ibid.

43. Ibid.

44. Ibid.

45. Myron Levin, "Smoker Group's Thick Wallet Raises Questions," *Los Angeles Times*, March 29, 1998, http://articles.latimes.com/1998/mar/29/news/mn-34044.

46. Ibid.

47. Ibid.

48. Ibid.

49. Ibid.

50. Ibid.

51. Dan Morain, "Assembly Panel OKs Tobacco Bill, Blocks 2nd Measure," *Los Angeles Times*, June 30, 1998, http://articles.latimes.com/1998/jun/30/news/mn-65020.

CHAPTER 7

1. Steven Mufson, "Coal Industry Plugs Into the Campaign," *The Washington Post,* January 18, 2008, http://www.washingtonpost.com/wp-dyn/content/article/2008/01/17/AR2008011702837.html.

2. Ibid.

3. Ibid.

4. Alex Kaplun, "Coal Industry Group Linked to a Dozen Forged Cap-And-Trade Letters," *The New York Times*, August 4, 2009, https://archive.nytimes.com/www.nytimes.com/gwire/2009/08/04/04greenwire-coal-industry-group-linked-to-a-dozen-forged-ca-2624.html?mcubz=3&pagewanted=all.

5. Ibid.

6. Mufson, "Industry Plugs."

7. Ibid.

8. Ibid.

9. Ibid.

10. Stephen Power, "Big Coal Campaigning to Keep Its Industry on Candidates' Minds," *The Wall Street Journal*, October 20, 2008, https://www.wsj.com/articles/SB122446094489848785.

11. Ibid.

12. Ibid.

13. Ibid.

14. Ibid.

15. Ibid.

16. Mufson, "Industry Plugs."

17. Kaplun, "Group Linked."

18. Ibid.

19. Ibid.

20. Ibid.

21. Jeffrey Ball, "Coal Hard Facts: Cleaning It Won't Be Dirt Cheap," *The Wall Street Journal*, March 20, 2009, https://www.wsj.com/articles/SB123751110892790871.

22. Ibid.

23. Ibid.

24. Ibid.

25. Ibid.

26. Ari Berman, "The Dirt on Clean Coal," *The Nation*, March 26, 2009, https://www.thenation.com/article/dirt-clean-coal/.

27. Ibid.

28. Ibid.

29. Ibid.

30. Ibid.

31. Ibid.

32. Ibid.

33. Ibid.

34. Brad Johnson, "Duke Energy Quits Scandal-Ridden American Coalition For Clean Coal Electricity," *ThinkProgress,* September 2, 2009, https://thinkprogress.org/duke-energy-quits-scandal-ridden-american -coalition-for-clean-coal-electricity-bdec8041fb23/.

35. Ibid.

36. Josh Harkinson, "No. 3: American Coalition for Clean Coal Electricity," *Mother Jones*, December 5, 2009, https://www.motherjones.com /environment/2009/12/dirty-dozen-climate-change-denial-02-american -coalition-clean-coal/.

37. Ibid.

38. Ibid.

39. Darren Samuelsohn, "'Clean coal' group downsizing amid industry struggles," *Politico,* September 28, 2015, https://www.politico.com/story/2015/09 /american-coalition-for-clean-coal-electricity-cuts-staff-214149.

40. Ibid.

41. Ibid.

CHAPTER 8

1. Pema Levy, "Alt-Right Movement Presents Its Vision for an All-White Society With Trump Paving the Way," *Mother Jones*, September 9, 2016, https://www.motherjones.com/politics/2016/09/alt-right-makes-its -main-stream-debut/.

2. Emily Jane Fox, "The Billionaire Father-Daughter Team Behind Trump's Apocalyptic Turn To The Alt-Right," *Vanity Fair*, August 18, 2016, https://www.vanityfair.com/news/2016/08/donald-trump-mercers -stephen-bannon.

3. Ibid.

4. Jane Mayer, "The Reclusive Hedge-Fund Tycoon Behind the Trump Presidency," *The New Yorker*, March 27, 2017, https://www.newyorker .com/magazine/2017/03/27/the-reclusive-hedge-fund-tycoon-behind -the-trump-presidency.

5. https://twitter.com/realDonaldTrump/status/832708293516632065.

6. Ibid.

7. Ibid.

8. Scott Patterson and Jenny Strasburg, "Pioneering Fund Stages Second Act," *The Wall Street Journal*, March 16, 2010, https://www.wsj.com /articles/SB10001424052748703494404575082000779302566.

9. Mayer, "Reclusive."

10. Joseph N. DiStefano, "When a hedge fund billionaire 'buys' democracy: Magerman on Mercer," *The Philadelphia Enquirer*, March 1, 2017, http://www2.philly.com/philly/blog/inq-phillydeals/Billionaires _and_Democracy_Magerman_Mercer_Renaissance_Trump_Bannon _Conway.html.

11. Ibid.

12. Mayer, "Reclusive."

13. Ibid.

14. Ibid.

15. Ibid.

16. Ibid.

17. Ibid.

18. Ibid.

19. Ibid.

20. David D. Kirkpatrick, "THE 2004 CAMPAIGN: THE CONSERVA-TIVES; Club of the Most Powerful Gathers in Strictest Privacy," *The New York Times*, August 28, 2004, https://www.nytimes.com/2004/08

/28/us/2004-campaign-conservatives-club-most-powerful-gathers
-strictest-privacy.html.

21. Mayer, "Reclusive."

22. Ibid.

23. Ibid.

24. Ibid.

25. Ibid.

26. Annie Linksey, "The Man Who Out-Koched the Kochs," *Bloomberg Businessweek*, October 22, 2014, https://www.bloomberg.com/news /articles/2014-10-23/the-man-who-outkoched-the-kochs.

27. Mayer, "Reclusive."

28. Ibid.

29. Ibid.

30. Ibid.

31. Alana Abramson and Lucinda Shen, "Conservative Megadonor Robert Mercer Is Stepping Down As CEO of His Massive Hedge Fund. Read His Full Statement," *Fortune*, November 2, 2017, http://fortune.com/2017/11 /02/robert-mercer-renaissance-technologies-breitbart-news-steve-bannon/.

32. Janet Lorin and Katherine Burton, "RenTech's Robert Mercer to Exit as Co-CEO, Sell Breitbart Stake," *Bloomberg Businessweek*, November 2, 2017, https://www.bloomberg.com/news/articles/2017-11-02/rentech -s-robert-mercer-to-resign-as-co-ceo-of-hedge-fund-firm.

33. Abramson, "Full Statement."

34. Ibid.

35. Ibid.

36. Ibid.

37. Ibid.

38. Oliver Darcy, "Robert Mercer says he'll sell Breitbart stake, distances himself from Bannon and Milo," *CNN Money*, November 2, 2017,

https://money.cnn.com/2017/11/02/media/robert-mercer-bannon-milo
-yiannopoulos-breitbart-letter/index.html.

39. Joseph Bernstein, "Hedge Fund Billionaire Robert Mercer Will Step
Down As CEO Of His Company Following BuzzFeed News Exposé,"
BuzzFeed News, November 2, 2017, https://www.buzzfeednews.com
/article/josephbernstein/hedge-fund-billionaire-robert-mercer-steps
-down-from-his#.hiVb5jKq1m.

40. Tina Nguyen, "'Holy S—T:' Allies Shocked as Bob Mercer Renounces
Milo, Dumps His Stake in Breitbart," *Vanity Fair*, November 2, 2017,
https://www.vanityfair.com/news/2017/11/bob-mercer-defunds-milo
-yiannopoulos-sells-stake-in-breitbart.

41. Adam K. Raymond "Robert Mercer, Billionaire Bannon Booster, Quits
Hedge Fund, Sells Breitbart Stake," *New York Magazine*, November 2,
2017, http://nymag.com/intelligencer/2017/11/robert-mercer-quits-hedge
-fund-sells-breitbart-stake.html?gtm=top.

42. Kyle Feldscher, "Robert Mercer: I regret supporting Milo Yiannopoulos and I'm cutting off his funding," *The Washington Examiner*,
November 2, 2017, https://www.washingtonexaminer.com/robert
-mercer-i-regret-supporting-milo-yiannopoulos-and-im-cutting-off-his
-funding.

43. Raymond, "Bannon Booster."

44. Rosie Gray, "The Mercers Wash Their Hands of Milo," *The Atlantic*,
November 2, 2017, https://www.theatlantic.com/politics/archive/2017
/11/the-mercers-wash-their-hands-of-milo/544877/.

45. Ibid.

46. Joseph Bernstein, "Here's How Breitbart And Milo Smuggled White
Nationalism Into The Mainstream," *BuzzFeed News*, October 5, 2017,
https://www.buzzfeednews.com/article/josephbernstein/heres-how
-breitbart-and-milo-smuggled-white-nationalism#.vtZABKgRD.

47. Ibid.

48. Ibid.
49. Ibid.
50. Ibid.
51. Ibid.
52. Ibid.
53. Ibid.
54. Ibid.
55. Ibid.

CHAPTER 9

1. "Oil Sands," American Petroleum Institute, accessed 2017, https://www.api.org/oil-and-natural-gas/wells-to-consumer/exploration-and-production/oil-sands.
2. Ibid.
3. Ibid.
4. https://web.archive.org/web/20110207192340/http://www.nebraskaenergyforum.com/.
5. https://web.archive.org/web/20180816084927/http://www.americasenergyforum.com/.
6. https://web.archive.org/web/20110207192340/http://www.nebraskaenergyforum.com/.
7. Kate Sheppard, "Oil Lobby Resorts to Twitter Astroturf to Promote Pipeline," *Mother Jones*, August 4, 2011, https://www.motherjones.com/politics/2011/08/twitter-astroturf-oil-keystone-xl/.
8. Ibid.
9. Lee Fang, "Yet Another Pro-Keystone XL Pipeline Front Group Set Up In Nebraska," *ThinkProgress*, September 7, 2011, https://thinkprogress.org/yet-another-pro-keystone-xl-pipeline-front-group-set-up-in-nebraska-864bb42ced71/.
10. Ibid.

11. Brian Merchant, "The Program Big Oil's PR Firm Uses to 'Convert Average Citizens'," *Motherboard*, November 18, 2014, https://motherboard.vice.com/en_us/article/xywmzk/a-top-pr-firm-promised-big-oil-software-that-can-convert-average-citizens.

12. Ibid.

13. Ibid.

14. Ibid.

15. Kate Sheppard, "Here's What Big Oil Has In The Pipes If Keystone Fails," *Huffington Post*, November 18, 2014, https://www.huffingtonpost.com/2014/11/17/transcanada-pipeline-oil_n_6174570.html.

16. Merchant, "Convert."

17. Ibid.

18. Ibid.

19. Ibid.

20. Ibid.

21. Ibid.

22. Ibid.

23. Ibid.

24. Ibid.

25. Ian Austen, "P.R. Firm Urges TransCanada to Target Opponents of Its Energy East Pipeline," *The New York Times*, November 17, 2014, https://www.nytimes.com/2014/11/18/business/pr-firm-urges-transcanada-to-target-opponents-of-its-energy-east-pipeline.html?_r=0.

26. Sheppard, "Keystone Fails."

27. Merchant, "Convert."

28. Jesse Coleman, Leaked: What you should know about Edelman and TransCanada's attack plan," *GreenPeace,* November 20, 2014, https://www.greenpeace.org/usa/leaked-edelman-transcanadas-pr-attack-plan/.

29. Ibid.

30. Austen, "Target Opponents."

31. Ibid.

32. Ibid.

33. Ibid.

34. Ibid.

35. Ibid.

36. Lisa Graves, "Edelman TransCanada Leak: Aggressive PR for Keystone Alt," *PR Watch,* November 18, 2014, https://www.prwatch.org/news /2014/11/12676/edelman-transcanada-leak-american-style-pr-plan -prepped-keystone-xl-pipeline.

37. Ibid.

38. Ibid.

39. Ibid.

40. Ibid.

41. Ibid.

42. Ibid.

43. Ibid.

44. Sheppard, "Keystone Fails."

45. Ibid.

46. Ibid.

47. Ibid.

48. Ibid.

49. Ibid.

50. Ibid.

51. Jay Michaelson, "How Canadian Oilmen Pinkwash the Keystone Pipe-line," *The Daily Beast*, December 28, 2014, https://www.thedailybeast .com/how-canadian-oilmen-pinkwash-the-keystone-pipeline.

52. Ibid.

53. Ibid.

54. Ibid.

55. Ibid.

56. Ibid.

57. Ibid.

58. Ibid.

59. Ibid.

60. Ibid.

INDEX